JAR *of* CLAY

LANE CARNES

Copyright © 2025 Lane Carnes.

All rights reserved. No part of this book may be reproduced, stored, or transmitted by any means—whether auditory, graphic, mechanical, or electronic—without written permission of both publisher and author, except in the case of brief excerpts used in critical articles and reviews. Unauthorized reproduction of any part of this work is illegal and is punishable by law.

ISBN: 978-1-63950-291-2 (sc)
ISBN: 978-1-63950-292-9 (e)

This publication contains the opinions and ideas of its author. It is intended to provide helpful and informative material on the subjects addressed in the publication. The author and publisher specifically disclaim all responsibility for any liability, loss, or risk, personal or otherwise, which is incurred as a consequence, directly or indirectly, of the use and application of any of the contents of this book.

Writers Apex

Gateway Towards Success

8063 MADISON AVE #1252
Indianapolis, IN 46227
+13176596889
www.writersapex.com

DEDICATION

THIS BOOK IS dedicated primarily to my estranged wife, Jan, for her love and support in allowing me to pursue my passion for writing. Secondly, Jan and I also want to devote it to the memory of our late cat, Garmo, who entertained us daily with her endearing personality. We will always remember her jumping and hanging from the outdoor screen in the living room when she wanted in at night. Garmo would also greet Jan with her coffee every morning on the dining room table stretched out in the folds of the daily newspaper. We often wake up and ask each other, "Where's Garmo?"

CONTENTS

Meditations on Mexico 1
Global Conflicts 14
Tripping 20
Oaxaca and Other Matters 29
Education, Immigration, and Racial Conflicts 37
Kayaking 47
Perspectives 52
New Orleans and Family 57
Mexican American and Politics 62
Clay and Languages 70
Venezuela and Salado Creek 73
A Bicycle Ride and Deep Thoughtfulness 76
Reparations and Liberal Democrats 82
America's Spiritual Challenges 84
The Dangers of Fundamentalism 89
Central American Gangs and American Ignorance 92
Riding, Triathlons, and Flow of Consciousness 101
A Third Political Party and the Ability to Speak Spanish 109
Jars of Clay 111
Conversations 115
Simón Bolívar 121
Latin America and Benito Juárez 123

Croatia and Puerto Rico 127
American Terror, Interpreting, and Isolation 131
Uncle Robert 136
The Catharsis of Writing 139
Iran and American Soccer 142
Family Dynamics and the Art of Conversations 146
Castro Points His Middle Finger at Latinos 149
Immigration and Political Discord 152
Bicycles and the Spiritual and Political Roads Less Travelled 157
World Citizens 164
The Molding of Clay and Thoughts 170
The Initial Dream 173

MEDITATIONS ON MEXICO

IN THE BEGINNING a vast emptiness prevailed. A ball of fire erupted dramatically from what appeared through the eyes of Rafael to be a volcano. Rafael awoke many times from this recurring dream. In the dream a princess evolved from the ashes of the fire once it subsided. She spoke to Rafael and said: "Dreams can only come true when we 'truly' believe." This surreal princess had beautiful long black hair, and she possessed magical powers and an indomitable will.

One day while Rafael was walking along the banks of the lush and pristine San Antonio River in Texas with his two friends, Sasha and Marcos, he shared his dream with them. It was a very bright and clear day. Birds flew and sang all around them. It was early spring, and the radiant glow of verdant plants surrounding them was especially visible. The brightness overshadowed the darkness he felt within. This dark mood was often triggered by this recurring hallucination.

Marcos was amused by his friend's illusion. Marcos was given this name by his Spanish father who was proud to be from Barcelona where the famous Salvador Dalí grew up and developed his craft becoming a famous surrealist artist. In the same vein of the renowned Spanish artist, Marcos couldn't stand the conformity of the conformist. Neither could he tolerate his father who had forced his *carpe diem* philosophy on him since his childhood. His father believed this maxim was part of his Spanish bloodline. According to his father, Marcos belonged to nobility because he was born and raised in Figueres, a town near Barcelona. He thought to himself, "Yeah, yeah... So, what?" All that metaphysical stuff preached to him by his father, a very proud Spaniard, was meaningless.

His father belonged to the "intelligentsia" of Spain, a group of intellectuals. Salvador Dalí with his "shellacked" mustache and the poet Federico García Lorca were members of this group. At least, Lorca stood up as a liberal rebel against the dictatorial forces of Francisco Franco during the Spanish Civil War of 1936. Unfortunately, Lorca was executed for his beliefs and opposition to Franco's regime.

Rafael, Sasha, and Marcos would often get together once a month and walk along the San Antonio River after eating a sumptuous breakfast. They usually ordered *migas*, a combination of refried beans, scrambled eggs with crumbled tortillas chips, and hot sauce served with fresh corn tortillas. After satisfying their appetite with their favorite dish and several cups of fresh coffee, the soft flowing river would seduce them into walking aimlessly along its edge. As they walked, they would often lose themselves in philosophical and spiritual discussions.

These discussions fueled many of the ideas Marcos incorporated in his works as a novelist. One day while he was sitting quietly at his desk working on a novel, his pen took him to a mystical place, a canyon surrounded by green valleys and endless meadows. Marcos sipped his green tea and thought about the towers, the horrific towers in New York. As he struggled to stay "conscious" in his world of nonfiction, he pondered many metaphysical subjects. He was literally lost in his own world of "magical" windmills, friars, and plain old cacti, like those depicted in the "no-account" novels of Louis L'Amour. From here his thoughts would contemplate Kant's *The Critique of Pure Reason*. Wasn't Kant the father of rational thought? Marcos liked to think that "reason was the voice of God speaking to man." Wasn't it, John Locke, the English philosopher who coined this philosophical maxim? Marcos's writing allowed him to drift into a subliminal dimension of consciousness where nations of the world would join together, where people would all speak the same "spiritual language," and where they would obey God.

As he printed his thoughts on the page in front of him, he remembered a trip he recently took to Mexico. While enjoying a cup of coffee in the courtyard of the Convent of San Francisco in Zacatecas, Mexico, he perused the collection of *máscaras* (masks), reflections in a mirror of Mexico's rich history. The crimson and pink stones of the courtyard protected the convent as the masks of the Mexican elites fooled the underprivileged and outside world. His mental labyrinth took him through the archives of a distant past that still existed in the melodies resounding from the saxophone of the previous night; they permeated the "ancient" walls of the Quinta Hotel, what used to be the old bull fighting arena. Now, the placid coolness of the night comforted his soul as he hid from the *maladies imaginaires* (imaginary diseases) of traditional society. Tradition, in the corrupt sense, where, for instance, the PRI (Institutional Revolutionary Party) was only a facade of corruptive and power hungry politicos reliving the *Porfiriato* maxim of *pan o palo*—either take the bread in the name of the Divine (Porfirio Díaz, the Mexican dictator) or you will be clubbed and killed. Politicos continued to hide behind the disguises of literature and its manipulative metaphorical deceptions, educating and entertaining themselves, but allowing the poor to suffer.

What would Don Quijote say about this abuse of power? What would José Ortega y Gasset, the renowned Spanish writer of the 20th century, say about this *esnobismo* (snobbishness) blossoming from the seeds of hypocrisy, especially, from the infected "seed" of the privileged who kept the common man blindfolded? "Es mejor la ceguera que la libertad creativa del pensamiento". (Blindness is better than the free and creative power of thought.) Marcos often thought to himself. Oh yes, Porfirio Díaz wanted to strut around in his official uniform, medals dangling like pompous weeds of power suffocating his own overblown ego. He preached, as if he were a sacred profit, "We, the people of Mexico, are so impressed with your fraudulent facade," these were Marcos's words. He could just imagine Porfirio trying to speak French in 1876 when he ruled Mexico. At this time, he welcomed the French bourgeoisie and their investments, which helped to finance his dictatorship. Monsieur José Limantour was his minister of finance. Marcos laughed at the thought of Porfirio trying to appear cultured as he mumbled some words in French. Marcos reveled in his meditative state as he thought about this nondescript dictator saying,

« Je suis le président génial de la grande République Mexicaine. » (I am the brilliant president of the great Mexican Republic.) Marcos thought to himself, "Yeah right! If you would have really understood the French, you would have read *The Social Contract* of Jean-Jacques Rousseau." It was the ideology that inspired the slogan, "Liberté, Fraternité et Démocratie" (Liberty, Brotherhood, and Democracy). Not only did it inspire the French Revolution in the 18th century, but it also inspired the Independence of Mexico and Latin America from Spain in 1810. It was here, in Zacatecas and Guanajuato, where Padre Hidalgo stood up against the *gachupines* (Spaniards) and their totalitarian ways.

As Marcos traveled the world, he felt a need to comprehend the secrets of life that corrupted man in the beginning. It all began, according to his interpretation of Genesis, when a gigantic eruption occurred and water fell from the sky, the land parted, and oceans appeared out of the breast of the earth. The chlorophyll and chloroplast of the plant life beneath the sea migrated and colonized the earth, much like man had done when he came from the Old World to colonize and enslave the inhabitants of the New World. In the name of the Church, he raped the native women and stole the wealth and riches from the Aztecs, Maya, and many other great Indigenous tribes. The colonizers ignored the ancient Chinese balance of Yin and Yang, which the Chinese would probably have ignored if they were the conquerors. Human nature always has its own way of messing things up. This whole concept of light and darkness, the conquerors and subjugated ones, female and male, and nature and God allowed man to make mistakes, but hopefully, he could correct himself by permitting the "divine vine" of life to intervene.

In Marcos's mind no man had to armor himself with superior weapons of destruction to subjugate the Indigenous people of these great lands. The melancholy of this situation prevails today in Mexico and in all Third World countries of the world. It's time for the powerful to humble themselves and evangelize themselves. In a fit of emotion, Marcos would often exclaim in Spanish: "¡Qué se evangelicen a sí mismos porque cuando 'evangelizaron' a otros no funcionó! La evangelización dio lugar a la esclavitud del hombre inocente, humilde y trabajador". (Marcos believed that the Spanish colonizers should have evangelized themselves because in the name of "evangelizing," they enslaved the innocent and humble working man and the Indigenous people of the New World.) What a shame that the noblest "evangelists" chose to ignore the rich parables, maxims, and beautiful metaphors depicted in the *Santa Biblia* (Holy Bible); what a shame that these noble ones turned out to be the most savage of men. It would be unfair to blame only the Spanish conquerors of these exploitations since there are numerous examples throughout history of men exploiting others and, of course, of Adam and Eve disobeying God in the Garden of Eden.

Sasha was often annoyed by Marcos's ruminations, his extrapolating tangents. One summer she accompanied Marcos to Mexico, and in the evenings they would often dine together at the Acropolis Restaurant in downtown Zacatecas, across the street from the theater. She always enjoyed a good discussion, and many of her ideas were influenced by Plato and the Greek thinkers. Aristotle interested her very much, especially his books: *Metaphysics* and *Poetics*. She was drawn by the logic of a written argument like a viewer is attracted to a marvelous painting. Marcos thought to himself again, "Man dialogues with himself constantly, especially when he is alone. He is attracted to the sensuality and eroticism of wine and love. Love is like a tragic sword used to drug man and to keep him enslaved to his temptations. Woman is like the bee that drinks the fruit of the most sumptuous flower. This flower blossomed from a prehistoric tree, the first tree ever created. It was under its shade where the first man contemplated his life. He frequently sat under this tree and thought about his existence as a "shipwrecked being" in a materialistic world. This extreme materialism is like alcohol overflowing daily from a glass drowning the "magic realism" of man's internal world. One is required to penetrate the shell of the hidden and disguised social fabric of a materialistic society where men drink to escape from their insignificance." Often, Marcos would overstate the obvious temptation afflicting many men. In a world of insignificance, men give in to their corrupt nature, whether it is their weakness for alcohol, women, and power.

According to Sasha, the lettered man should teach the masses with his own mouth and money to raise society from its ignorance and poverty, a society in which there is a lack of schools. This is what Miguel Cané, the well-known Uruguayan writer and educator, wanted to do in the mid-19th and early 20th centuries. However, the opposite has occurred since the upper and middle classes have received the best education while the poor, who are in the majority, have received no education. By keeping the poor and Indigenous people of Latin America uneducated, the upper classes have been able to rule over them. The poor have been literally kicked and treated as *perros satos* (stray dogs). We are *La ciudad de los perros* (*The City of the Dogs*) as the 21st century Peruvian writer, Mario Vargas Llosa, describes in his novel. The upper classes are protected by dictatorships and the military, which are often referred to as *perros*, as well. What happened to the words of José Vasconcelos, the 20th century Mexican philosopher, who talked about the importance of mixing the races in his novel *La raza cósmica*? Why isn't the Black man from Mexico referred to as African Mexican? Didn't Jesus Christ have dark skin? The African Mexican is just as important as any other race. Does the *gachupín* (White Spaniard) think he is the God of Mexico and the rest of the world? Doesn't he see God in his own reflection as all men do? Didn't he read *Way to Wisdom* by Karl Jaspers, the 20th century German writer, who believed that the philosopher like man should constantly be searching for God's truth? The philosophical man is different from some ministers, fathers of the Church, who know they have found God, and they no longer yearn to search daily for him. However, the philosophical man searches for him daily.

Martin Luther King Jr., Gandhi, Mother Teresa, and others preached "philia"—love among men.

Many in the Church, especially, the leaders have left their "spiritual arms" unattended, much like Don Quijote, who when realizing his "dream" of becoming a *caballero noble* (noble gentleman), found his rusty and oxidized weapons: shield, helmet, sword, and lance. He realized it was time to polish them to prepare them for his many adventures and battles. To all the fathers, ministers, and people of the Church, who have lost their "path to wisdom," Sasha pleaded with them to return to the path of truth, not the trail of racism and segregation. May God and humanity, especially the "philosophers," the true seekers of truth, teach others to search the unconscious world to tap into the essence of love, innocence, and the will to cherish and protect all human lives from the evils of racism. May the wells of the soul never dry, and may the thirst for justice and truth never be quenched. This was Sasha's dream for humankind: "Please accept the *philia*, and live and die by it under all circumstances."

Rafael was attracted to the outdoors. The music of the world embroiled with sounds of nature: birds floating from tree to tree, landing precariously on the mirage of a glass surface of a lake or pond. Independent of the material indulgences of man, he sat in silence pondering the curvatures of a blade of grass or the silhouette of a tree beaming in the sun. So often, he thought, "we" miss the simple things in life. He knew man was consuming himself with noise and the stress of modern day living. The need to exhaust oneself into oblivion was the common creed. He mocked society and man for its shallowness. His grandfather, Feliciano, once told him that tranquility is the pillar of peace, and it is like a small pebble sinking and drifting through the molecules of water creating concentric circles of calmness.

As Rafael contemplated life, Marcos took off on a mysterious trip to the far away land of Guanajuato, Mexico, an enchanted land dominated by humble people before the Spanish or *gachupines* arrived with their pompous armor of terrorism, lies, and deceits. Rain fell from the sky right before dusk; *perros satos* ambled the twilight hours of early dawn. It was their home, now, that the chosen ones slept and drowned in their own drunken state. The *calles* (streets) were silent. Humble vendors prepared their *carritos de venta* (vending carts) for the long day. It was just another day to earn a daily wage. Was it the *pan* (bread) of Christ, or was it the bread of the dictator, Porfirio Díaz, who tried to control this country in 1876? Who was Díaz trying to fool with his "máscara" (mask), pretending to be cultured and to care for his people? Just because he spoke a little French and because he could quote one or two of Montaigne's thoughts: « Il qui ne doubt pas est très stupide. » (He who doesn't doubt is very stupid.) These were Marcos's words, pretending to be Montaigne. Porfirio believed he was an intellectual. Wow, Marcos was so impressed by this *títere* (puppet) and his other cohorts, like Limantour, his financial advisor, who helped Porfirio and his army steal and rape the *mestizos* (the mixed race created between the Spanish and Indigenous blood), the poor people of Mexico. I'm sure Porfirio was serving his god, his ego.

Marcos sat pensively at the Valadez Restaurant in downtown Guanajuato. Bells rang in the background as the infamous *payaso* (clown) in his humble street clothes entertained a small audience on the front steps of the Teatro Juárez de Guanajuato. He had long hair, and the young people surrounded him as they enjoyed the humorous show. Art frees man from all things, all worries, and concerns. Marcos loved art because it allowed one to exist in the moment, in which a person could simply be. Children naturally live in this state of being until the reality of life weighs in on them. Learning to let go amidst the responsibilities of daily life is truly a gift that everyone needs to afford themselves as they become adults.

On another occasion Marcos reminisced about attending a church service on a Sunday morning. Inside the cathedral a world of splendor decorated in gold served as a backdrop for a clergyman giving his sermon. The attendees listened as the words circulated through the air creating a sharp contrast between the believers inside and the poor Indigenous woman sitting on the steps in front of the cathedral holding a child. Both were hungry and desperate. This paradox paints the portrait of Mexico, a country that has had difficulty meeting the needs of the poor. It's a country dominated by the corruption of the PRI (Independent Revolutionary Party) that has monopolized Mexican politics since the end of the Mexican Revolution in 1921. It is a self-serving political party that only meets the needs of the elite and powerful. In this unstable economic and political environment, the cartels have also flourished creating a market for illegal drugs and crime. But not only is it a paradox for Mexico, but for the world since the poor are often neglected in even the most economically stable countries, like the United States.

Rafael realized that rarely do things change. His thoughts shifted to the previous night when he found himself walking among the labyrinth of small streets of this great city, Guanajuato. Guanajuato in English means "frog." This association reminded him of the *coquí*, probably one of the smallest frogs of the world that inhabits the island of Puerto Rico. It lives primarily in *El Yunque*, a well-known rain forest with a plethora of waterfalls, in the mountainous area of the northeastern side of the island. Rafael was always fascinated by animals living in their natural environment, a place where the fittest survived. Now, his thoughts made him think of the turtle, especially to the meaning the Chinese attributed to this animal. The turtle's shell has five indentations or separations, eternal symbols of the flow of existence. Again, these were his ideas. Rafael thought of this existence as the multiple layers of the heart, which protect its core where the fountain of love originates.

This morning, at an hour right before dawn, Marcos and Rafael left the Diego Rivera Posada Hotel, located 100 meters from la *Alhóndiga* that reverenced building of the Mexican Revolution. *Padre Hidalgo* initiated the *Grito de la Independencia* (Call for Independence) in this building, a historical treasure, on September 16, 1810. They ran for about forty minutes climbing a road leading up a mountain until they arrived to the precipice overlooking the valley where Guanajuato was nestled. At the peak of these mountains, the mystical nature of the city dwelt amidst the natural beauty of its surroundings. The crimson colored rays of the new day only magnified the moment with its picturesque panorama.

Later that day, as Marcos was writing and drinking a cup of coffee at the café in the *Biblioteca Insurgente* in San Miguel de Allende, Mexico, he overheard a disgruntled *gringo* (American) who complained about paying ten *pesos* for a bottle of water. The man said in English, "Are you crazy? I can buy a bottle of water for five *pesos* down the street." Two thoughts entered Marcos mind as he contemplated the situation. For one, a bottle of water would cost approximately 20 *pesos* in the states, and it was interesting that the American was speaking to the clerk in English instead of Spanish. The silence of the clerk clearly agitated the foreigner more. Marcos could not understand the American's impertinence as he thought to himself: "Why visit Mexico, and expect a reduced monetary value for everything? And, why couldn't the foreigner attempt to speak Spanish?" On a very small scale, according to Marcos, this was an example of the insensitivity of many tourists when they visit a foreign country. From another perspective these types of value systems lead to wars and conflicts of a much more serious nature.

His thoughts return to a daydreaming state with his pen sliding on a blank page. The Franciscan father hides between the green bushes of eternal silence, praying while he kneels on the rock embedded floor containing blue tiles from Saltillo, Mexico. There is a round bronze table surrounded by chairs of black iron. The dripping fountain humidifies the ambiance, which is muffled by the noise of dishes being placed in a dishwasher. Walls of stone and red stucco sustain the cement and black mud from the soil of this café. In the background of this holy patio, the slapping sound of a waiter unfolding a tablecloth and placing it over a round table can be heard. The elaborate table is the product of a hammer used by a skilled worker. Singing bells awaken the birds at ten till six. Carpets of leaves grow on the stone wall, and the roof resounds like tablecloths with each bell strike of the wind, harmonizing with the clinkering noise of a car passing nearby. The water from the fountain soothes and calms Rafael. A total chaotic chasm from the wind sways between the clear green leaves shaped like the *flamboyán*, but without its red flowers. The fierce force of the maddened wind can be heard as the policeman blows his whistle creating a stark disturbance that penetrates the narrow, angular, and long streets. The bird's resonance vibrates in between the water's concentric circles falling as a holy blessing on the pavement. A yellow flower blossoms in the center of two trees, the very two painted by Diego Rivera in his first painting. It germinates like a yellow mermaid, standing with a golden hue in between those two angular wooden structures climbing onto imaginary steps to the second floor of this holy place. Rafael and Marcos sit and observe curiously. Marcos feels the presence of a sexy angular woman with a cigarette in hand who, like the goddess Diana, tempts man by offering him wine from fermented grapes. An elephant plant extends itself in front of some black and white photographs encased in frames, one containing an unlit candle—a symbol of the present, the only "time" we have. Other images abandoned in the library by a reader. Books without an audience, inanimate objects, and letters rest on a blank page. A smile of an unknown man enriches a painting with vibrant colors. A *quetzal* bird flies in between two eternal hills warmed by a red moon that only knows an anguishing pain. Four silver coated rings encircle a huge clay jug. From its epicenter, two green bushes grow with a dark red glowing fire on the walls of its leaves. Marcos feels peaceful, and the smile of his transcendence rebounds against the opposite wall from where he is seated. It is seven minutes past six, and the bells awaken them from this magical dream on their first day in San Miguel de Allende, Mexico.

Marcos remembered Sasha was reading the book *Indigenismo* by Henri Faure. She was sunbathing next to a cascade of a natural waterfall, idyllic and almost Amazonian. Each morning she would awaken at daylight to practice yoga and meditate. She learned yoga from Melissa, a good friend. Now, Melissa lives in San Miguel de Allende, this beautiful international town, almost mystical, of bohemian people. At night one can hear the melodies of "Guantanamera, de cualquier malla sale un ratón, oye, oye".

Salsa music and other Latin American classics emanate on the clay roofs creating a harmonious sound in unison with the cars, cell phones, and voices heard in *Rosario*, a restaurant known for its good service and humble waiters here in San Miguel de Allende.

Sasha was drying herself with the golden towel of the sun. She was thin like one of those Barbie dolls, an invention of North American beauty. Her breasts were perfectly round due to silicone implants, and her skin had a bronze hue. Her curvaceous figure resembled that of a gorgeous mermaid lost in the depth of the Atlantic. Her black hair like a dark starless night rested on her shoulders like two wild doves. More than anything, her eyes reflected brilliantly in the mirror of blue clear seas where one could see the undulating circles of a strong emotion for life. It was a clear morning, and the blueness of the sky penetrated her eyes.

What bothered Sasha about Faure and the other fools like Darwin and Spencer is that they were racists like Auguste Comte, an atheist who invented *Positivism* to enslave the Indigenous people. With science and industry, the Positivists wanted to drown them in the waters of miscegenation. José Vasconcelos, a Mexican thinker and philosopher, viewed the miscegenation of the European with the Indigenous races as a significant process in creating a strong ethnic group. Nevertheless, the Europeans and anthropologists who do not believe in God, like Robert Redfield, and others, like López Portillo y Rojas who wrote *La raza indígena*, maintain that the Indigenous population does not want to be like the Europeans. He expresses this view by stating: "[N]o he conocido a ningún indio en México o en ninguna parte que se quiere asociar con el europeo ateo, científico, industrial—ni para nada". ("I have not known an aborigine in Mexico or in any other part who wants to associate with the European atheist, scientist, and industrialist— not for anything.") Thinking quietly to herself, Sasha believed that this pompous, avaricious, and inferior European ignored the metaphors and the windmills of Cervantes, of Don Quijote. His ego consumes him like the alcohol consumes the man who does not look within as recommended by the Spanish author, Ortega y Gasset. These dogs like Carlos Salinas (ex-president of Mexico), Trujillo in the Dominican Republic, and Leopoldo in Argentina always stole from the people. Dictators like Fidel Castro, Somoza, Noriega, and many others also did the same.

Many Latin American dictators and professors inculcated by the ideology of Che Guevara hide behind their elegant intellectual cloaks. They do not fight with arms but with the Platonic dialogue of education. Their subliminal Marxist and theological arguments do not oppose those of Saint Augustine, Thomas Aquinas, or the pope. These dictators and professors twist the thoughts of Augustine, Aquinas, and the Church to fit their agenda, in which they usually blame the West and capitalism for the ills of their countries.

It just so happens that the pope is visiting Mexico today, July 30, 2002. He is perambulating around in his papal mobile speculating on the importance of the cultural, racial, and economic unity among the Mexican population. It is interesting to note that while the pope and other visiting dignitaries visit Mexico and stay in the most luxurious hotels with sumptuous meals, the Indigenous people, mostly uneducated, of this great country are dying of hunger at the door steps of the cathedrals in most towns in Mexico. The Mexican people are tired of the rhetoric. What is needed are more schools, hospitals, good jobs, and a political system that is not corrupted by power and greed.

Meanwhile, Rafael sat on the steps of the *Diego Rivera Posada*, and he contemplated the sign *Paso al Tiempo* (Passage into Time). He also observed the house dog barking at passing cars, people walking by, and the wall. It seemed like the dog only barked, as Puerto Ricans would say, "*para hacerse el aguaje de creerse malo*" (to pretend to be bad). Since Rafael considered himself to be somewhat of a philosopher by nature, he became interested in the personality of the dog. While this street dog, with a long tail and cropped brown-white hair, was lying on its left side with its right sharp-pointed ear hanging loosely on the side of his head, he seemed aware of his villainous appearance. Watching this eccentric dog was very comical. At that moment, Rafael took advantage of the quiet laziness of the dog to pull out from a bag fifty wooden sticks to practice the ritual of the *I Ching*, the Chinese book of Change. He separated the sticks into groups of four, five, nine, and other numbered stacks. Only 49 sticks were separated because the first one was used to begin another survey. This was his interpretation. Rafael had always been a meticulous student of the great works of Western philosophy, but he grew tired of Descartes and John Locke's ideas that prophesized: "I think therefore I am, and reason is the voice of God in man." Eastern philosophy was beginning to interest him because it seemed to be based less on the rationalism of Kant and other western thinkers and more on the subconscious, spirit, and intuition of man.

Rafael had two new friends, Jesús and Marta. They were the owners of *La Posada de Diego Rivera Inn*, and they were very passionate about work. They were painting the walls to the entrance of their inn a brownish-yellow color. Rafael was fascinated by the way they manipulated the sponges in their hands creating a beautiful texture of color on the wall. They appeared to be in a meditative state as they painted since they worked quietly and systematically. According to Leonardo Da Vinci, the hand was the most versatile part of the human body. Even though Rafael was not completely certain, he believed Da Vinci made this observation. Rafael was never concerned with exact details or quotes from authors, artists, or others he read about since he surmised that most thinkers borrowed ideas from others. He believed Da Vinci and others, like Michael Angelo, would sit under a majestic tree, created by their imagination, to contemplate the mysteries of life. This reminded Rafael of the movie, *A Beautiful Mind*, which he saw a few weeks ago while his dog Mohawk was lying by his side on a comfortable rug. It was about a boy who had autism and lived in his own world. As a writer, Rafael understood that solitude was essential in order to create. Could the boy's solitude fuel his imaginary world as well? Mohawk seemed to soak it all in sublimely as he twitched in his sleep. Being a Rhodesian ridgeback with a crest of hair growing backwards on his back, he must be reminiscing about the past, in which his ancestors chased lions in Rhodesia, Africa. This breed would keep the lions at bay while the hunters on horseback closed in on the lions, cornered by large rock formations, or nestled in the trees above the dogs. The speed and agility of these dogs were formidable.

GLOBAL CONFLICTS

RAFAEL'S THOUGHTS SHIFTED to events of September 11, 2001. He thought about the jihadist leaders like Osama Bin Laden and the late Saddam Hussein. Whether September 11th was orchestrated by men like Osama Bin Laden or not, Rafael had difficulty understanding how a group of individuals could fly into the twin towers killing hundreds of innocent people in the name of Allah. It was Rafael's opinion that Maimonides, the Jewish thinker from Spain, would be extremely disappointed with Osama and his extremist group. The Muslim influence was very predominant in Spain from 711-1492. According to Rafael's recollections, Maimonides believed in God and Allah, and nowhere in his writings did he preach hatred and the extermination of other people. El Cid, the liberator, along with the Catholic Spanish authorities defeated the Arabs in 1492. In other words, the Arabic reign was over, and Spain became a Spanish kingdom under the reign of Queen Isabel and King Fernando. The remnants of Arabic influence are still evident in places like the Alhambra, the Arabic palace, which still exists in Granada, a city in the southern part of Spain.

The confusion occurs because there is not an appropriate dialogue between leaders like Osama and others from the Arabic and non-Arabic world. Not being a student of the Koran, Rafael could not understand the attack of September 11, 2001 on innocent people. However, Osama did get the attention of the West by committing these acts of terror. The results of these attacks are portrayed in the battlefields of Iraq and Afghanistan. In Iraq, according to Rafael's limited knowledge, the civil strife between the Sunnis, Shiites, and other tribes has always existed but now is exacerbated. It seems like these tribal warfares will continue unless the leaders of the Arab nations agree to gather together and discuss the issues that divide them. If Muhammad believed it was important to inflict war upon all the nations and people of the world, who are infidels and do not honor Allah according to his definition, the leaders of all non-Islamic countries are facing a real threat. There is no doubt that the Christians of the Middle Ages did the same during the Crusades as they punished or killed any heretic who did not follow the doctrines of the Catholic Church. One must not rule out the harsh treatment of the Black slaves in the United States by many Christians, which led to the Civil War of 1861, but fortunately, slavery was finally abolished at its conclusion in 1865 even though racial tensions still exist in America.

All of these digressions led Rafael and Marcos to believe that the problems in the world stemmed from greed and a lack of understanding among cultures. The world has finally moved from one of isolation to one of unity in the sense that each country is dependent upon each other. The Internet and travel have allowed mankind to visit and conduct business with each other. Nevertheless, the downside of our technological world is its inability to value philosophy, history, languages, and all world religions in an effort to become more tolerant of one another and to care and reduce the separation of the powerful and rich from the less fortunate and poor. The moral codes of societies have corroded. Many countries like the United States are seduced by a materialism creating an appetite that is never satisfied. Children grow up wanting fancy cars, clothes, and jewelry. The significance of finding a job that is meaningful is nonexistent. The value of seeking happiness and living in harmony with one's fellow man and nature is hypothetical. The Romantics made a point by living simply and intentionally. They did not invent a new form of living because this form of living was created by Christ. Christ lived simply, and he preached from his soul. He was not a famous academic who published books that no one read and are stored away in libraries and covered in dust. Christ's word is real. Unlike Sartre who placed his faith in existentialism; in other words, he trusted man. Man is a contradiction; therefore, he can't trust himself. Salvador Dalí, the famous surrealist painter from Figueres, Spain, was creative because of God. Dalí is not God. His ideas were not special. Dalí reacted against a materialistic Spain, one that valued fascism and the control of the masses. He reacted against the materialism of the West, but he did not give credit to Christ because he was reacting against the Catholic Church, which was corrupt. At least, this was Marcos's opinion. Marcos and Rafael both believed the pope is not Christ, the incarnate. They agreed the pope was a man with a divine calling; he should be respected for the guidance and love he provides to his fellow believers. The pope does not sit in a higher seat than any man. The pope disseminates the word of God, and he serves as an example for men to share God's word with one another.

The French thinker Jean-Paul Sartre was a great intellectual because he had the courage to think and question the significance of life. All men should think and ponder the existential and spiritual aspects of their lives. It is our nature, even though it is often ignored, to question these philosophical issues. Sartre wrote *Being and Nothingness*; thus, as implied in the title, life is a paradox. To be is to live and trust in God. It is possible that Sartre did not confess a personal belief in God. Nothingness predominates when man alienates himself from God. Was its Sartre's belief that nothingness stemmed from man's inability to think deeply? What Sartre may have not realized is that man thinks because God gives him the thoughts to do so. When one submits himself to a higher being, life flows more fluidly. This concept associated with the movement of water, according to the Greeks and other ancient civilizations, is a strong force, one that renews the soul. This is possibly why people were baptized with water because it renews the spirit. The undulating flow of the ocean fills the rivers of the world and of life. Man cannot exist without water since it is his source of life. It emanates from the heavens, and God created the water and oceans in Genesis at the inception of time. In Revelations it describes the river of life that will inundate the world. It's important to speak allegorically and metaphorically about the images of life. Gabriel García Márquez, in his novel *Cien años de soledad* (*One Hundred Years of Solitude*)*,* stole this idea of magical realism from the Bible. He did not invent anything new as he created this fictitious town in Latin America called Macondo. All poets, especially David, the author of Psalms wrote figuratively. Metaphors come from God. He is the creator of all arts, all thoughts, languages, and cultures.

Men live in a material world in which they are controlled by money and the freedom it brings. Freedom comes to those who free their hearts from the desires of materialism. It is expressed in the natural wonders of nature when a person views a river or the waves of the sea "joyfully" lapping the soft sand of the beach. Freedom is given to those who travel and learn other languages in order to get to know other people of the world. It comes to the artist who paints freely without attempting to be recognized, and it is experienced by the writer who writes in order not to be read by others. He doesn't write for fame, but he writes as a catharsis for understanding himself and his thoughts. Freedom is not the result of earning millions of dollars, but it is derived from those who live passionately. It is the gift God gives all people, and it is our choice to accept or reject it freely.

As Sasha and Marcos travelled the world, they noticed that man struggles against himself and those who were in a position of power. The powerful, like Mr. Alejandro Toledo, the president of Peru, cared only about filling their pockets with money at the expense of the poor people who can barely make a living. People, like Hugo Chávez, the president of Venezuela, who painted a few homes for the poor; then said, he was helping them. However, he neglected to help create more jobs and social benefits for them. Many presidents in the United States, like Mr. Bill Clinton who is a Rhodes scholar, lacked the ability to speak a foreign language. This language skill might have helped when dialoging with politicians and leaders of other countries. People in these positions should be reminded that they are servants of humankind. Inadvertently, this could be one cause of terrorism in the world. It is a disguised terrorism, which is not as radical as one that promotes killing innocent people, but it is one that evolves from the fallen nature of man.

Marcos often pondered the suffering of the world. Being far from Iraq, it was impossible to truly understand the struggle of that country. Logically, it seemed evident that a tyrant like Saddam Hussein could not be tolerated. Saddam Hussein created a country of inhumane suffering. People were tortured and killed if they did not submit to his rule. At least this is the image portrayed of him in the United States and other countries around the world. Could it be possible to really know unless one lived and experienced life in Iraq? Oil money received from other countries was used to build up Hussein's arsenal of bombs and weapons. Since Iraq could not prosper because of the sanctions imposed on its country, it would find other means for obtaining money to promote its cause. The people of Iraq were suffering because of this improper spending of money. A person could not live freely, and truly realize his dreams under these conditions. Saddam blamed the Western world for its poverty and alienation. He used religion to condemn the United States and its Christianity against the Islamic world. Iraq controlled its own media; therefore, it was easy to disseminate false information about the outside world. Saddam knew that if he could control the thoughts of his people, he could rule unopposed for a very long time. Iraq became a haven for terrorists and fundamentalists that opposed and easily blamed the Western world. Rafael knew this was one view of Iraq, and the mistake would be to consider it the only perspective.

The Western world was at fault as well since its knowledge and understanding of Iraq and other Middle Eastern countries was very limited. The United States, for example, is isolated by its language and culture. The Middle East is far away, and most Americans do not frequent this part of the world because, for one, they don't speak English in the Middle East. And, secondly, most Americans do not know much about the Arab world. Conversely, one could say that most Arabs do not know much about the United States. It fascinated Marcos that our modern world was so advanced in technology and sciences, but we were still so far behind in communicating and understanding people from other countries. He often pondered whether a country like the United States could ever completely understand countries like Iraq and Afghanistan.

One was the language barrier, there is no doubt, but another, Marcos believed, was the materialism that consumes most Americans and people from developed countries. Most Americans like all people in the world work to provide for their families and personal needs. Their responsibilities take up much of their time, and they are very practical because they see more value in learning skills that will enhance their working capabilities. For example, most Americans choose to learn more about computers to perform their work more efficiently and effectively. It is more difficult and more alien to learn another language because, for one, it takes a lot of discipline and the monetary value does not pay off quickly. Yes, Americans are interested in oil for their automobiles, and they are interested in doing business abroad. However, these interests are material interests because they enhance their pocket book, which provides them with the means to travel and to buy. It's hard to develop a spiritual need for learning about others. It's much easier to give donations to help the starving people of the world, and to fund organizations that fight for the civil rights of all people. It's a spiritual problem that affects all people, not just Americans. Many times the United States and the Western world are blamed the most because these countries have the material means that allows them to prosper and live a rather peaceful life. These countries have experienced living in a democracy that allows people to work, think, and live freely. Nevertheless, the United States is experiencing its own economic woes in 2011, and it is a nation whose people also suffer from poverty.

Rafael stretched slowly on his green and rectangular sofa. He was meditating on Tolstoy's novel *The Cossacks*. After reading a paragraph, he elapsed into a somnambulant fit of laughter from one of the incidents in the story. One of the characters was walking along a trail; this is where Rafael rewrote the script by referencing an event that took place in his hometown. He saw two trees that had fallen due to the recent floods of the Guadalupe River in Canyon Lake, Texas. Two cypress trees, hundreds of years old, fell like giants painted by the pen of the author. Cypresses, carrying in their veins the genealogy of the past years, which still exist in the present of their outer banks. Rafael, conscious of the present, tried to remain in the present much like his cat, Lucy. It seemed to him that man is inferior to animals because of his capacity to reason, forcing his mind to drift aimlessly between the past, present, and future. Reason confuses him like a cloud covering a crescent moon, smiling behind a curtain of fog, shipwrecked like a vessel without a destination. This was the image causing him much laughter as he contemplated his own enslavement created by this thoughts. Life could be much simpler if man could master the ability to focus more readily on the present, but this is where the paradox lies. Man lives in a broken world, and he himself is broken. All humans suffer from this satirical affliction.

TRIPPING

RAFAEL THOUGHT OF this affliction when he married Josefina years later on April 4, 2014. After a year of marriage, he became very bellicose after working for a year and a half teaching Spanish at a middle school in South Texas. They had known each other for five years before marrying. He was disgruntled from work since it took a toll on him because he worked 13-14 hours a day. Furthermore, he was an avid athlete, so he would bike, run, swim, or lift weights after teaching all day. When he did get home at 8 or 9 p.m., there was only time to shower, watch a little TV with Josefina, and go to bed. He often quarreled with Josefina as he complained about a kid at work who may have told him "fuck you" on a particular day, or an administrator who allowed a student to return to class after he dismissed him. Trying to find a balance between disciplining and teaching became overwhelming, which only added fuel to the fire when he came home. She would try to understand but many times would say, "Maybe, you could be a little more loving." Rafael was too heated to really listen to her advice, and it only triggered him more believing she was siding with the child or administrator.

Josefina referred to that year in April 2015 as the year Rafael "was tripping." One week after Rafael was given a few days of leave from the school due to an incident involving a disciplinary act with some students, he decided he wasn't going to return to school to discuss the issue with the superintendent and principal. That evening after a heated discussion with Josefina, he decided he was going to leave. When he tried to pull out of their driveway in San Antonio, Texas, Josefina stood in front of his truck preventing him from leaving. He then got out of the car and began to walk away to the nearest hotel about five miles away. It was about 10 p.m., and he arrived to the motel at about midnight. He came home the next day, and things worsened between him and Josefina. He began to call her names and demeaned her Catholic faith. There is no doubt his ego got the best of him. He quoted from the Bible to attack her faith and beliefs. He left again, and this time he packed some clothes and brought his Edward Jones and Frost Bank checkbooks with him. They would not see each other for approximately five months, and Rafael wanted a divorce at that time.

This was a critical point in Rafael's life, one that intertwined with his search for meaning as he shared his turmoil with his friend, Sasha, over those difficult months of separation from Josefina, the love of his life. Sasha was reading the book *The Doctor and the Soul* by Viktor E. Frankl, the famous psychiatrist who spent years in one of the German concentration camps during World War II. Those who survived the harsh conditions were the ones who were able to set goals. They could envision being released from the camps at a determined time in the future. Others hoped to be reunited with their loved ones at some point. Dr. Frankl was motivated to finish his book. He would write the main ideas to his book on scrap paper or any other material he could find so that he could reconstruct his story. It was hard for Sasha to imagine what life in those concentration camps was like. Just imagine working ten hours or more in the barbarous winter conditions of Europe with little food and insufficient clothing. Being an athlete, Sasha understood the importance of diet and nutrition for fueling the body to withstand the hardships of riding a bicycle for fifty miles or more or running ten miles. Many times she would feel totally depleted. But the real test would have been enduring life in one of those concentration camps. The days must have seemed endless, and the monotony would have been difficult to overcome. Dr. Frankl discusses the responsibility each man had to take care of himself. Each person had the duty to get up each morning and eat whatever food was provided, so he could work each day. There is no doubt that men and women, who survived these camps, like Dr. Frankl, were able to face their suffering with courage, and they were bold enough to set a goal for their future to survive. Unfortunately, those who did not set goals died.

Sasha often discussed issues of this nature with Marcos and Rafael. Man's isolation from others in today's society causes much pain. The pain is probably not as severe as being subjected to the hardships of a concentration camp, but nevertheless, the pain is real. Marcos shared with Sasha the difficulty of finding a soul mate. He had been married twice, and these failed marriages had caused much pain in his life. Recently, he just ended a two year engagement with his fiancée. Love is a complex human emotion that can bring two people together joyfully, but it can also lead to much pain. Marcos and his female partners became too intimate in a short period of time, which would cloud the relationship. He would feel an obligation to get married, or to have a serious liaison once the love making began. It was hard to control this part of the relationship. He knew it was important to avoid making love until marriage. This was a difficult barrier for him to transcend. He discovered that once you cross this barrier, one often overlooks the differences and incompatibilities between yourself and the other person. This can cause much pain because one feels responsible to that person. You try to work through these differences, but the doubt and pain remains.

Rafael had fallen by the wayside spiritually when he left Josefina. Everything he believed and practiced as a Christian, knowing perfectly well his imperfections, was now disregarded. The following day, after leaving Josefina, he went to a Toyota car dealership and bought a small 2004 white Kia for $5,000.00. After the purchase he drove to New Braunfels, Texas where he stayed for one night in a Super 8 Motel. He was energized by his will and need to be right. Years later, he realized the pain he caused himself and Josefina. He loved her so much that he could never see this happening again after they got back together. At the time, he believed Josefina was trying to control him much like his ex-wife had done, and he didn't want this to repeat itself. He didn't realize it at the time that he was the one who created much of the friction by his lack of sleep and his inability to see his anger and frustration objectively. Josefina's love and devotion to Rafael proved stronger in the long run. It would take some time before he was able to remain still and silent again to be able to listen to God's voice.

Sasha agreed with Rafael and Marcos that many times we separate ourselves from the divine love of God and allow our egos to control our lives. Recently, she watched *The Realm of the Senses*. It was a Japanese film about a prostitute who is employed as a servant at a prominent Japanese household. She immediately engages in a sexual relationship with the master of the house who is married. They engage in sex throughout the whole movie. They are seeking a permanent state of pleasure and desire, and they are fulfilling this desire. As Sasha watched the film, she realized how sex in our world had truly lost any meaning. It is pleasurable, but when two people seek gratification only, it eventually destroys a relationship. At the end of the movie, the lady cuts off the man's sexual organ. They had become involved in masochistic sex because they needed to experience pain to enhance their sex. They were avoiding the natural emotional affliction of living. This agony is evident in the hardships we, as humans, experience in life as it relates to our faith, our jobs, and ties with other people. If we seek a life of pleasure without torment and suffering, we will only find misery. Pleasure only leads to discomfort. This is not to say that a healthy relationship between a man and a woman is not pleasurable. God intended for men and women to have such a relationship. But God also intended for men and women to worship him first. As humans we must conform our way of thinking to his image and not to our way of thinking.

Marcos agreed with Sasha, and he believed that many times people rush into relationships because of their own loneliness. There is an inherent fear of living alone for the rest of one's life. Man has to continually wrestle with his alienation and come to terms with it. What must it have been like for Christ on the night before his crucifixion, knowing that he was going to endure the death on the cross the next day? As a human, he felt very lonely. This type of loneliness only Christ could bear because he was the Son of God. God gave him the strength, and Christ was able to face the pain and responsibility of his death. This was the ultimate gift given to mankind. Christ died on the Cross for our sins, our loneliness, and our despair. Christ's death is so metaphorical that it confuses the mind. The mind and its limitations cannot possibly conceive what Christ did for us by dying on the cross.

Eventually, Rafael stayed for two weeks at a Courtyard Marriot Hotel in Seguin, Texas. He purchased a trek training bicycle since he was an avid triathlete. He had left all of his cycling gear behind, so he also had to buy biking shoes, a helmet, pump, and cycling clothes. He truly concluded his relationship with Josefina was not going to work out. He had brief conversations with Josefina over the phone, but they turned into shouting matches more than anything. He blamed her for his misunderstandings and failures at work. Josefina listened but also attacked him by suggesting he see a psychiatrist. It was turning out to be quite an expensive ordeal for Rafael since he had also hired a lawyer to represent him. Rafael believed he was harassed and treated unfairly at the junior high where he was teaching Spanish. Luckily, he was still being paid by the school district, and he was also collecting rent money from two homes he owned. The money allowed him to cover the unexpected costs.

Although Rafael was lost spiritually at this time, he realized that Christ was the answer to all the problems we face. This relationship with Christ is the most difficult one to develop. Man must trust him in a world that denies him unintentionally when the ego gradually takes control. We must trust Jesus by getting up each morning with a smile on our face regardless of the situation we are confronting.

Rafael often became frustrated in his own life with all of its complexities. The stress of teaching young kids, many who were not interested in learning, was a heavy burden. The constant discipline problems were disheartening, and it became difficult to find pleasure and a purpose in his work. In addition, he felt like he wasn't growing intellectually because he was not reading or writing very much. Many times he faced a wall, and he didn't know how to get over it.

Christ preached and instructed us to love all children and to care for them. We are all products and children of God. Rafael knew his attitude had to change. He needed to conform his mind to God's way of viewing things and not to his. This attitude transcended into his workouts. As a triathlete, there were days when he didn't feel like running, swimming, or biking, but he persevered and forced himself to workout. He knew he was struggling to keep Christ at the center of his life each and every day. Rafael often wondered about the meaning of life for himself and others. Our days are full of chores and tasks, pertaining to our work and the things we do with our leisure time. We often go from one task to another, which many times becomes a mindless routine.

Then, consider how all of this extends out into the world. We live in a world where there are real concerns like poverty, disease, war, death, and a multitude of suffering. We live in a world where people are Buddhists, Hindus, Jewish, Islamic, Catholics, Christians, atheists, and hedonists. We have to develop our own individual faith, but we cannot isolate ourselves from others. We live in a world that is getting smaller and smaller. Our world is very diverse where people speak different languages, worship different gods, and live under different conditions with various challenges. Politics is an arena that we cannot ignore. If the Islamic extremists want to make the world conform to their ideology by means of terrorism, we must, as a world, confront this serious threat. These terrorist want to return to an era where their language, literature, and lifestyle were the dominant way of life. Iraq used to be the center of the world as far as knowledge and learning were concerned; it wants to return to this golden age of predominance. We must learn Arabic and Farsi as well as other languages in order to understand each other. Christ would want us to love and accept one another as well. Rafael concluded that we cannot continue to allow our selfish desires and goals to insulate us from the woes of others.

Sasha, Marcos, and Rafael often discussed the meaning of life. Victor Frankl definitely explored this theme in his book *Man's Search for Meaning*. It was incomprehensible to Sasha and Marcos to try to imagine the extremes of the concentration camps. Each prisoner was stripped of all of his personal possessions, and they were also forced to shave all the hair from their bodies. They were basically naked. At night, nine men shared a makeshift bed made of wood with two blankets but with no mattresses or pillows. If men could not withstand the workload, they were sent to the gas chamber. In addition, they did not have proper clothing or shoes.

Each man owned one pair of pants, one shirt, and one pair of shoes, which often had holes in them. Hope kept most of them alive. They envisioned eventually getting together with their loved ones. Victor hoped to finish writing his manuscript of his lifelong work. His wife and all of his family members were extinguished in the gas chambers.

These men and women endured an enormous amount of pain and suffering. According to one minister, who Marcos listened to on the radio, man should really suffer more than he normally does. The act of Christ dying on the Cross for our sins forgives man from his sins. We actually do not deserve to be forgiven because of our sinful nature, but Christ saved us. Just imagine what life would be like if we were not forgiven by Christ. Life would be unbearable. It would be a constant hell. God, in his mercy, redeemed us from perpetual afflictions. What we endure in life is minimal compared to the suffering we would experience if Christ would not have died on the Cross for our sins.

This great act by Christ for us was undeniable, but we can still ask questions regarding all the distress in the world. Innocent people like Mr. Frankl endured many hardships along with many others: whether it were the Blacks during the years of slavery in America from the early 17th century until 1865, the terrorists attacks of 9/11, the recent attack in New York on 10/31/2017 by a driver who claimed allegiance to ISIS and plowed down innocent people on bicycles, and the countless other events of the past and present. Yes, Rafael and his friends agreed that man is a sinner, but why all this tragedy and death if Christ died for our sins. This is the question that boggles the mind of mankind.

Harold S. Kushner attempts to answer this question in his book *Living a Life that Matters*. He describes the importance of our unspiritual and spiritual lives. The unspiritual existence is the one where we compete and achieve to find meaning. This life satisfies the ego; thus, it provides some meaning but leaves one feeling empty. The spiritual life is one of compassion and love towards oneself and others. It is here that man finds the fulfillment he needs when he establishes a close relationship with God. This is not an easy relationship to foster in a world of diverse religions and faiths. We are all subjected to imposing our world and spiritual views on others, which separates us from one another. Many Christians ascertain that Christ is the only way while Islam prefers the lessons and leadership of Muhammad, for example. There is a vast number of beliefs and religions in the world. The concept of God is impossible to place in a crucible that defines all of man's convictions throughout the world. There are some common themes among all faiths, such as: love one another, live in peace with your brother, and forgive each other. These are just a few of the maxims that are cornerstones of all religions.

Rafael and Josefina agreed on these principles of their Christian faith even though they had some slight differences. Josefina was brought up as a Catholic, and Rafael was raised in an evangelistic church setting. Neither one of them were die-hard fundamentalists in their beliefs. They both believed in God and accepted Jesus Christ as the Son of God who died on the Cross and was resurrected on the third day. They didn't force their beliefs on others, and they tried their best to be compassionate and loving towards one another and all people. However, Rafael needed to practice these principles now that he was experiencing a challenging trial with his work and relationship with Josefina. In a microcosm, this was an example of man failing to honor God, and Rafael did not succeed in this area. Neither was he practicing the biblical principles towards his wife, which define love as kind, patient, and forgiving. Rafael was blindfolded by his anger and selfishness, which overshadowed these Christian principles.

Understandably, he realized, now, that Josefina became frantic because of his actions and behavior towards her. He allowed the external problems related to his work to interfere with his spiritual life and peace of mind. It would take approximately five months before he realized his mistakes and humble himself before God. Josefina showed him unconditional love throughout the whole ordeal, and there was no doubt she proved God's love towards him. She served as a beacon of God's faithfulness, compassion, forgiveness, and love towards him. This was a lesson he would never forget, and the experience drew them closer together spiritually.

Sasha agreed with Rafael that it was hard to keep Christ at the center of our lives. There are so many distractions that pull us away. One of the many distractions is pleasure. Many times people escape from suffering by submerging themselves in the traps of pleasure. Think about all the strip clubs that exist. Places that many men and women frequent. They seek to fill a void in their lives and hearts because they feel lonely. She believed in Christ, but often it was really hard to really understand his love for us. It was difficult to have the kind of faith that would fill the bottomless abyss rather than exposing oneself to the temptations of the flesh. Sasha knew what it was like to feel the erotic pleasures of intercourse and sex. These were temporary pleasures that were not long-lasting. She had been married twice, and both of her marriages failed. She believed Christ was not at the center of those relationships. Since her divorce six years ago, she has been engaged twice with her last engagement lasting two years. She was torn between the pleasures of sex and waiting until she married. But there were other factors to consider. Her partner was a Christian and had an extended family. It seemed like much of their time together centered on his family. She felt smothered at times and became very ambivalent about the prospect of getting married.

Marcos understood her dilemma because he knew that human relationships were challenging. Man is scared of being alone, so he searches for a mate to keep him company and share his dreams. Since man is a social being, there is an inherent need to love and to be loved. This is what Christ wants for all of us. Many times it's difficult to choose a partner because man chooses to satisfy a need that only God can fill. Once this emptiness is replaced by God's love, man is in a better position to choose a mate for life. Marcos admitted that many times man refused to allow God in his life, and without this divine guidance, it is difficult to love someone completely with one's heart, soul, and mind.

He thought about this one night when he went *salsa* dancing by himself at a local restaurant and club, called *Pasión,* in San Antonio. It had been several months since he had broken up with his girlfriend. He became frustrated because, in a sense, he was seeking a replacement for his girlfriend. He thought it would be easy to meet someone while he was dancing. But it felt very uncomfortable to be at a club by himself. He explained to Sasha that he danced a couple of times, and he tried to carry on a conversation with these women. He sensed they were not interested in talking. He felt a little discouraged and lonely. In a way, he was glad that he broke up with his girlfriend because she wanted more of a commitment from him than he was willing to give. He missed talking and sharing things with her. However, their conversations were devoid of intellectual meaning, lacking substance, and any form of curiosity. Marcos respected her too much to continue having a relationship with her without giving himself totally to her.

OAXACA AND OTHER MATTERS

SASHA, IN THE meantime, was sitting on the hidden beach of Puerto Escondido, Mexico in the state of Oaxaca. The ocean was lapping softly on the compacted sand at twilight. Oaxaca was and is primarily populated by Indigenous people who are primarily descendants of the Zapotecs and Mixtecs. Things were slow to change here. People still lived off the land growing their small crops of corn and frijoles with a multitude of herbs and grasses. The lifestyle was slow in contrast with the fast pace of the *chilangos*, the residents of the more industrious and progressive people of Mexico City. Oaxaca was probably one of the poorest regions in Mexico. Seventy percent of the Mexican population lives in poverty while thirty percent belong to the higher echelon of society.

While daydreaming, she remembered her conversation with Rafael a month earlier when he rented an apartment in Canyon Lake, Texas during his separation from Josefina. His apartment was on top of a long-inclined hill, which gave him an unobscured view of the Texas Hill Country. From his balcony on the third floor, he could see another hill to the north in its natural state with plenty of cedar and oak trees. Rafael was glad to be back by the lake, and the apartment was brand new. However, the toilet did overflow his first week as a female tenant flushed sanitary wipes in the commode. The pipes from his apartment were connected to those of his neighbor directly across from him on the other side of the complex. There was an obstruction on the bottom floors that was causing the problem. It was a nasty experience because when the toilet was removed, all of the backed up excrement flowed all over the floor of the bathroom. He purchased several rolls of paper towels and bought an industrial type mop to clean up the mess. It was not fun.

Rafael made friends with the neighbors even though it felt awkward to be living in an apartment again after residing in a home for most of his adult life. He realized he had isolated himself from Josefina while teaching at the junior high school. The long hours and the difficulty he had adapting to the disciplining of the students became a burden. Now, he recognized he had some issues to face and overcome. As an athlete, he felt it was necessary to push through these difficulties. Sasha could relate to Rafael's feeling of isolation, and their conversations were helpful for both of them.

In the meantime, Josefina was reading and listening to Marianne Williamson, a spiritual coach, who became well-known through her teachings from the book *A Course of Miracles*. Williamson grew up in Houston and experienced her own search for meaning during her younger years. Now, she lectures and conducts conferences across the United States and internationally on the principles of love and spirituality. Williamson seeks to bridge the divide between all religions by underscoring the commonality they share. Letting go of the ego is one of the main entrapments that affects all humans. Many of us define ourselves by our accomplishments. Not only did Josefina have to remind herself of how the ego encourages her to try to control aspects of her life and others, but Rafael had to also be aware of how his ego interfered with his ability to love more freely.

Rafael had just finished reading *Born to Run* by Christopher McDougall, and he was impressed by the Tarahumara Indians from the Copper Canyon area of Mexico. These people are super athletes who run 40-50 miles on a regular basis with sandals made from the rubber of automobile tires. They enjoy running in groups, and it is believed they run to hunt for food.

They live a quiet and sequestered existence in the treacherous canyons where it is easy to fall to one's death due to the prevalence of rocky cliffs.

They have endured the test of time ever since the Spaniards learned about them in the 16th century.

As a runner for approximately forty years, Rafael had to slowly but reluctantly accept the fact that he was getting slower as a runner. He would always remember running a 10-mile race in about 58 minutes, just under a six-minute pace. He could also recall running the Austin Marathon in 1992 and finishing with a time of 2hr 49mins. At the age of 59 in 2017, he knew those days were gone. His personal record for a one-mile run was 4mins 47secs, which took place more than twenty years ago. He has not run under a seven-minute mile in a few years now. It was challenging for him not to dwell on slower performances. This was the ego measuring his success or failure as a runner based on time. As a triathlete now for the past twenty-five years, he realized that running had to be balanced with swimming and biking whereas before, he just ran. Obviously, he wasn't racking up the miles running as he used to do. He was learning to let go and accept the course of life, knowing that we are all moving closer to death with each passing year.

According to Teresa Pruett, Sasha's friend and a native of Mexico City, the Indigenous people want to be left alone on their small portions of land. Teresa stated there was an overall indifference among the tribes regarding education. The majority of the Indigenous people were satisfied with eating, being among family, working the land, and hunting. Their view of politics was very insular, demure, and isolationist.

Furthermore, Teresa did not understand terrorism and al-Qaida. To her it appeared the U.S. bombed and infiltrated Iraq for no legitimate reason. Sasha was completely amazed by Teresa's opinion. Saddam Hussein, a heinous murderer of the Kurds, Shiites, and any other ethnic groups opposing him, was destabilizing the country with his extremism. Iraq was the breeding ground for terrorism, an extreme form of Islam that wanted to destabilize the Middle East and disseminate its evil to all four corners of the world. If the Middle Eastern insurgents, who cowardly flew into the twin towers on September 11, 2001, had not attacked the U.S., the invasion of Iraq and Afghanistan would not have transpired. Actually, this heinous attack should have aroused all free nations to rally and join in combating the extreme form of terrorism that seeks to blame the U.S. and Western Europe for their failing totalitarian forms of government. The terrorist want to establish a world where the upper echelon of government is controlled by a few leaders and aristocrats while women are suppressed into second class citizens, and where children are brainwashed to believe that all industrial Western powers are the fruits of Satan and of his plan to devour them.

Sasha was very concerned by Teresa's indifference, one that was reflected in the government of Mexico, primarily dominated by one political party, PRI (Partido Revolucionario Institucional), which controlled Mexican politics with corruption, deceit, and the manipulation of the poor masses for more than 70 years. A government in which past presidents like Salinas, Zedillo, Echeverría, and others stole millions of pesos from the Mexican people to fill their pockets and their lecherous needs. Teresa's indifference towards world politics was an ingrained insouciance to Mexican politics. If this nonchalant attitude predominated among the majority of the Mexican population, those in power could continue to subjugate the poor. Sasha believed it was important to denounce this type of subordination, much like Buddha did when he spoke against the injustices of the Brahmins, the ruling class of the Hindus. Jesus did the same when he opposed the strict traditions and rituals of the Pharisees and privileged Jewish leaders who placed themselves above the general population.

As Sasha sat at her table, a barking dog refocused her attention on the serene ambiance surrounding her, and the notes emanating from the Indigenous pan flutes in the background swayed her in the early evening hours. The moon was three-quarters full, and its resplendent light bounced off the shadows of the fishing boats anchored in the calm lakelike water standing about 200 feet away. She would continue to contemplate Mexico's natural beauty as well as its polemical political status, especially now that she was sitting under an umbrella in the midst of the tranquil activities of the Zócalo, the main plaza. She survived a seven-hour bus ride through the serpentine roads of the Southern Sierra Madre Mountains. There was only one stop prompted by the urgency of a mestizo woman wanting to use the restroom. Sasha and the other passengers took advantage of this stop to go themselves and stretch their legs. She was slightly repelled by the lack of sanitation; afterwards, she realized she had to dip a bucket from a nearby barrel to fill it with water to top off the toilet in order to flush it. This was a typical task in the abundantly impoverished communities that barely existed on the outskirts of major cities like Oaxaca. This substandard existence was the result of an oppressive government that lived lavishly as it enslaved the less fortunate in the guise of a democratic society.

After arriving to Oaxaca and settling into a substandard motel, Sasha jointed Marcos in the late afternoon for a sumptuous meal of *fajitas de pollo* with corn tortillas. Marcos also ordered a bowl of vegetable soup and a large fruit plate, consisting of fresh pineapple, papaya, watermelon, and cantaloupe. It was a delightful meal. Afterwards, they ambled along the shadowed-filled streets of the colonial town. Long shadows cast themselves over the Saltillo tiles and rock paved streets of this bustling Indigenous town. Merchants filled the streets and the Zócalo with a plethora of colorful handwoven baskets, shirts, dresses embroidered with ripe flowers, necklaces, and bracelets hung from wood perches, and brightly painted wooden fish floated in polychromatic spirals from timbered sticks attached to fish string. The colorful circus was silenced when Marcos entered one of the many colonial churches to observe its enduring internal architecture with its Doric beams and arches. The silence of birds chirping in the highest dome resonated throughout the massive temple filled with a multitude of candles sitting on igneous tables casting their light and shadows on the patron saints of the Catholics. The Virgin of Guadalupe is the primary matron saint of this town and the rest of Mexico. Marcos did not relish the saints and statues of this grand temple, but he absorbed the silence of the chamber, a peaceful calmness representative of the reticence one finds within. The cathedral was a place of escape from the bustling noise of everyday life. It represented the trees in the forest that provide shelter from the sun where the rain only filters the necessary drops for sustaining life in its most fundamental physical and spiritual form.

Sasha was anticipating her break from teaching junior high students as the Christmas holidays of 2007 were quickly approaching with six more days of school left. She was looking forward to travelling with her boyfriend to Baja California for a few days of reflection, rest, and recovery. She felt sorry for those who did not realize the importance of leaving one's town and state in order to meditate upon the deeper meaning of living. We constantly have to remove ourselves from "our box" to see life as it is really meant to be lived.

After reading an article in the *San Antonio Express-News* about the interest Iran was showing in building a dry canal through Nicaragua, now that Daniel Ortega regained the presidency of this Central American country, Marcos thought about world politics. Iran was aligning itself with many leftist regimes in Latin America: Ecuador, Bolivia, Venezuela, Nicaragua, and the Tri-Border Area of Paraguay, Brazil, and Argentina. The Hezbollah terrorist group from Iran has been active in this border region. What concerned Marcos was the United States' neglect of these areas in Latin America. This region could be pivotal in maintaining a world balance between terrorism and an anti-terrorist campaign. America's basic inability to dialogue with Latin American cultures in Spanish was crippling. Without the ability and willingness to speak Spanish, America was basically incapable of understanding the political undercurrents of these Hispanic countries. For example, the Rama and Creole Indigenous populations of Nicaragua live on the political margins of this country often being ignored and neglected. Many live in the Monkey Point Community on the Caribbean coast, and they fought alongside the Contras, supported by the United States, during the guerrilla warfare against the Sandinistas led by Daniel Ortega from 1980-1988. Many of these Indigenous people are trying to claim their legal rights to much of the land in that area. However, other regions of this poor country in the Western Hemisphere are ready to align themselves with a terrorist regime like Iran, which is developing uranium enriched energy for nuclear arms, because they want jobs for their people. The U.S. has had an opportunity to invest and possibly help Nicaragua emerge from its ashes of scarcity, but because of a lack of foreign language skills, primarily Spanish, and economic interest in other areas of the world, America has ignored its neighbors to the South. Evidently, the energy of the American military and political institutions have been consumed with the war in Iraq for the past seven years where there is also a clear rift between cultural understandings. Again, the inability of the American society, diplomats, and military advisors to learn and speak the exact Arabic dialect of the Iraqi people is evident. This lack of language skills keeps America on the outskirts and fringes of truly comprehending the conflict in Iraq and other areas of the world.

Learning other languages is not cost effective, and the amount of time required to master a foreign language is an area where most American institutions do not want to allocate their resources and time. In our schools across the nation, foreign languages are not considered part of the core curriculum dominated by math, science, English, and history, the main subjects taught in each school. However, viewing how small the world is becoming each year, it seemed completely blasphemous to Marcos not to extend the same level of importance to foreign languages. There was no doubt in his mind that foreign languages should be as important as the core subjects. Learning a foreign language is instrumental in relating to people of other cultures. There must be a willingness to communicate and to assess the needs of all people around the globe. It is certain that love for one another is important, but the question becomes how one expresses this love directly to others. With an international community that is receptive to communicating in multiple languages, there is a better chance for properly monitoring political leaders who might abuse their powers in order to enlarge their bank accounts. The ones who suffer the most are the poor and less fortunate who succumb to the greed of the powerful and to nations that isolate themselves from others through their entrenched monolingual indifference to other cultures.

Marcos and Sasha often discussed the issues of the Middle East from an outsider's perspective. After the recent upheavals in Egypt and the current events in Libya, it is interesting to note the unity displayed by the common people of these countries who have gathered together to oppose Muammar Gaddafi. Gaddafi is a multi-millionaire who owns hotels and businesses in many countries in Africa. By dethroning this ruthless dictator, many would lose their jobs since they are employed in these hotels, banks, and other institutions. There is much at stake because it is not just a matter of incarcerating Gaddafi. Marcos pondered these issues as he sat outside of his home in Canyon Lake enjoying the dim light of dusk fading in the distance. A cooler breeze had engulfed the area after a torrential rainfall saturated the ground after almost 40 days without any rain. Wildfires were rampant in many parts of Texas and Arizona. Marcos often wondered how Americans or anyone for that matter could concern themselves with issues in other countries when they have to deal with matters that are more imminent. For instance, Marcos many times was consumed by hustling to obtain teaching assignments from semester to semester as an adjunct instructor. How could he dedicate himself completely to his writing with this constant search for classes? He did not enjoy a stable working condition, and he had to pay his own health insurance along with trying to save money for retirement. In Arizona people are dealing with wildfires and the possible threats of their homes burning down. In these cases, how can they fully comprehend the intrinsic and political nuances of the Middle East, North Korea, or China? Yes, learning foreign languages would help to penetrate some of these cultural layers, but how do school administrators deal with limited budgets and larger class sizes. These are complex issues that require much thought and examination.

There are millions of refugees fleeing Libya, Syria, and many other nations across the world afflicted by conflict and war. How do the developed nations like the United States, France, Germany, and others help? The United States is experiencing almost 8% unemployment, and Americans are fighting a protracted war on two fronts, in Iraq and Afghanistan. The war in Afghanistan has lasted approximately 18 years, and much of the deficit is due to the expenses pertaining to this conflict, not to mention the thousands of lives lost. Sasha wondered whether it was fair to totally blame Barack Obama for the woes of the economy and the war. Is pulling out of Afghanistan the answer? Sasha did not think this was the answer since the Taliban had a free hand at ruling and oppressing the people of this ravished country. Helping the police and military of Afghanistan to take control of their own problems seemed like the most logical answer.

Sasha remembered that later in the week she was going to meet Rafael and Josefina for dinner at Soluna, a trendy restaurant on Broadway in San Antonio. Rafael recently told her he had started working as a Spanish interpreter for Worldwide Languages, a small company in the area. He really enjoyed the part-time job since he was semiretired. They would contract him several times a week to translate for parents attending their annual special education evaluation, the ARD (Admission, Review, and Dismissal) meeting at local schools, and for patients at a hospital or clinic who did not speak English.

EDUCATION, IMMIGRATION, AND RACIAL CONFLICTS

RAFAEL WAS HAPPY he was no longer teaching. In his opinion schools and their administration were run like big businesses; as a result, they were less supportive of teachers. This created a harsh environment for teachers to work effectively with their students. More and more responsibility was placed on teachers for the failure of their students. Students and parents should be held more accountable for their roles in the academic process. It was hard for Rafael to explicate his disdain for the public school system. Being in the classroom day in and day out with the same kids for a whole year was nauseating. Adolescents were experiencing their individual ups and downs as they searched for their own identity with themselves and their peers. Even when Rafael would teach in a creative manner, creating songs and short videos with his cat, Garmo, many students dismissed his efforts by talking and misbehaving. Plus, students did not want to create their own songs or videos unless they were enrolled in an upper-division class, like an advanced placement course or a college credit class.

Schools have drifted away from the Socratic method. Socrates was an enigmatic philosopher whose life spanned from 469-399 B.C. He lived frugally, and he was materially independent due to an inheritance he acquired. He was a citizen of Athens, and all Athenians received state subsidies, such as theater passes. It is known that he was an ugly man with bulging eyes, a stub nose, belly, and a squat build. He was almost 40 years old at the outbreak of the Peloponnesian War of 431, and at this time he became a public figure. His intellectual development can only be inferred by learning the natural philosophy of Anaxagoras and Archelaus. He also experienced the teachings of the Sophists. But neither method appealed to him because natural philosophy did not help man's soul, and the Sophists questioned everything, which was the basis for establishing new knowledge or denying the validity of all tradition.

Socrates did not create a new doctrine. He did not believe he was a prophet who needed to tell men about God. Nevertheless, he realized his mission was to be among men, himself included in this group. His purpose was to question everything and to realize that man's "self" only resided in the knowledge of what's true and good. He demanded each individual to question, test, and refer to his own self for the truth. Socrates believed in the polis and laws of Athens, and he abided by them even if they were unjust. But he firmly supposed that truth could only be found in questioning and thought, and it could only be defined by each man or woman.

Sasha wondered where the public schools had failed. Schools rely too much on the state curriculum and essential skills students need to know to pass from one grade level to the next. Within this academic framework students are required to be the recipients of knowledge instead of creators of enlightenment which they could acquire for themselves through dialogue and questioning. Unfortunately, students were still memorizing information to regurgitate on exams. Students are not given the freedom to extrapolate information to spawn their own conclusions and perspectives.

This method of biliousness can be observed in many church services as well, especially in the Catholic Church, which adheres to a strict protocol. There are always three readings from the Bible: one passage from the Old Testament and two from the New Testament. These are followed by a homily given by the priest. The exhortation is usually a verbatim explanation or recapitulation of the third passage. From Sasha's experience of attending Mass, ninety-nine percent of preachments lack any substance. There is very little ascertainment, critical, or creative thought. There is no added intellectual food for thought in regards to the gospel. There is no reference, for example, as to why Nietzsche believed God was dead. Sasha believed he was referring to the corruption of the Church back in the 19th century where clergy directly influenced kingdoms and their political, social, and economic institutions. There is no mention of the naturalness of man questioning his faith as suggested by Miguel de Unamuno, the Spanish writer, philosopher, and theologian. There is no reference to Thomas Aquinas, St. Augustine, Socrates, Plato, or Buddha, for example. Yes, the sermonettes are centered on God's word, work, and the life of Jesus Christ, as they should be. But there is no critical thinking as it relates to the rich biblical passages. People during the Enlightenment, the Romantic Period, the Renaissance, and other ages struggled with understanding God's word. People today also wrestle with the meaning of God, but there is little or no reflection of substance that feeds the people. Could this be one reason people are leaving traditional churches?

As Sasha and Rafael had these political and philosophical conversations over a warm cup of coffee, they mused over the present caravan of immigrants travelling through Mexico on November 2, 2018. They were marching from their native countries of Honduras, El Salvador, and Guatemala where gangs, such as the Mara Salvatrucha (MS-13) and Barrio 18 created havoc by extortion, violence, and a multitude of other criminal activity. Juan Orlando Hernández, the current president of Honduras, was corrupt and has been known to divert millions of dollars given in aid from the U.S. to award those officials in power by providing them with benefits and rewards. This money was allocated by the U.S. to help Honduras, for instance, to improve its security institutions, such as the police and military to combat the drug cartels and gang related activities. The money was also supposed to help build more schools so that young people could be prepared to enter the work force, which would reduce the amount of youths recruited by the gangs. In addition, the money was supposed to be used to create more jobs and improve the legal system, which currently does not have the infrastructure to prosecute and convict criminals. The impunity of criminals, corrupt politicians, and police officers is rampant in these three Central American countries formerly mentioned.

This creates a huge immigration problem for the U.S. since many are forced to leave their countries in search for a better life. The young people only have two options: to immigrate north or succumb to joining a gang to earn a living. Others immigrate due to the exorbitant amount of money they must pay gangs to operate their business or just for residing in their neighborhoods. If they don't pay the extortion fee, they along with their family members could be murdered. U.S. policy has ignored many of these chronic problems since they are interested in maintaining the Palmerola Air Base, a Honduran military base, which houses between 400-600 American troops. The U.S. military uses this base to fight the war on drugs and for humanitarian aid to Central American countries.

President Trump refers to this caravan of Central American immigrants as a massive invasion of the U.S. since there are about two thousand of them marching towards the American border. He is preparing approximately 1,000 military troops to meet them at the border between Mexico and the U.S. This is another reason why he is so adamant about building a wall to keep illegal immigrants from entering the U.S.

Rafael observed that the immigration problem was not only about building a wall or not, a position that both Democrats and Republicans debate vehemently, especially now, during the primary elections of the fall of 2018. There should be more pressure applied not only to the government of Hernández in Honduras, but also to the corrupt officials governing in El Salvador and Guatemala as well. There is not enough done diplomatically to impose sanctions and persuade these Central American countries to change and end the degeneracy.

As a first step, the U.S. could stop sending millions of dollars in aid to these countries. Or, at least, establish agencies in these territories controlled by the U.S. and other international countries, such as Germany, Spain, and France, to coordinate and manage how these funds would be allocated for rebuilding an infrastructure to improve the educational system as well as the security and legal institutions. But the inability of the United States to deal effectively with these Central American countries pertains directly to the general misunderstandings of the American citizens of the conditions in these regions. This was exemplified recently when Rafael and Josefina were attending an annual family gathering in Nags Head, North Carolina when some of their relatives stated: "Of course it's necessary to build a wall along the border of Mexico and the U.S. Have you noticed that the caravan of immigrants include primarily young men? Yes, they want to bring corruption and violence to our country." They no longer wanted to discuss this issue with Rafael when he suggested it was necessary to place more pressure on the Central American governments to do more for their people so they won't immigrate in the first place. People have difficulty listening to a point of view that differs from their own, and it is one reason Americans have been more divisive.

Rafael wondered where this abhorrence to discuss and dialogue came from. Why do so many people think their truth is the only credibility in political, philosophical, and religious discussions? Josefina believed it was because most people isolated themselves in their own families, communities, and country. We as humans prefer to associate with others who have similar views as we do. It is uncomfortable to meander beyond the borders we create for ourselves and those with whom we commune. In part, our schools should provide more opportunities for forums in which people from diverse political, social, and cultural backgrounds are able to discuss their views in a civil and respectful manner. Schools are still structured around the teacher who pontificates and the students who listen. Politics are structured around the Republican and Democratic Parties, which prefer to distance themselves from one another with opposing views in which many times they refuse to reach an agreement for passing bills into laws, whether this pertains to immigration, environment, or social issues. Gridlock seems to be the order of the day.

Rafael speculated whether the younger generation would be equipped to deal with the complex issues we face as a nation and as a global community. The dichotomy of technology and the internet, which unifies the world in some regards as far as information is concerned, but separates and disengages many from one another with their computers and smartphones, which are prioritized over relationships with other human beings. Many spend more time communicating on social media than they do conversing and interacting with those in their immediate surroundings. Why does this happen? What has gone wrong in our society? Why are we attracted to alienation? Many times, Rafael would gather at a nearby Starbucks with Marcos, Sasha, and his wife to discuss these problems. As humans we like the warmth of a robust cup of warm coffee in our hands as we detach ourselves in the stream of our technology with soft playing music and the sound of coffee beans grinding in the background.

Sasha felt like money was the main culprit. Universities have become institutions for many to obtain degrees and not knowledge necessarily. The drive is to get a degree in medicine, law, engineering, and other disciplines in order to make money to buy and consume the "American Dream," which includes the big home, a nice car, clothes, and comfort. Politicians seek life terms in office to further their agenda and to cement their legacy and financial security. There is nothing wrong with financial security, but it seems to outweigh and blind people from truly communicating, sharing, and caring for others. Our government sends young soldiers to war in places like Afghanistan where we have been at war with the Taliban for 18 years. What did we learn from our failure in Vietnam? What have we really learned about the Taliban and their culture? How can the American people discuss equal rights for women with the Taliban? These are questions that remain unanswered, and they are the reason wars and conflicts persist in these areas of the Middle East. What do Americans really know about Russian politics and culture? Can we as a nation or world ever reach a complete understanding of these conflicts that divide us?

After taking a sip of his tall latte with whole milk, Marcos thought about those Americans who travelled abroad on a regular basis, preferring to visit places like Cancún in Mexico or Punta Cana in the Dominican Republic where they are catered to in English in a resort environment. On the other hand, those who speak other languages and venture to foreign lands with an interest in meeting the people they encounter and visiting their museums and other historical sites may develop a better understanding of the dissimilarities that divide their countries. It's possible they acquire a tolerance for divergent customs, points of view, and traditions that vary from their own. As a result, their total identification with being solely an American or Spaniard, for example, begins to change and morph into the concept of being more of a citizen of the world. Their view of themselves within a global concept becomes more amplified. Travel is the key for making this transition from indifference and ignorance to understanding and fomenting a broader scope of political and cultural views.

Sasha recalled a recent conversation she had with a relative in Arizona on a visit there this past summer. Her husband's nephew was talking about his college classes, and one thing led to another. One of the deliberations centered on blaming the White-American male for many of the problems in society. Most White males were presidents and CEOs of businesses. Men like Harvey Weinstein, a Hollywood producer, sexually abused female actresses, which led to the Me Too Movement where women began to speak out against the abuse by White male bosses in positions of power. It was common for universities to bash the White-American male, and this also became a predominant theme espoused by the Black Lives Matter movement, which primarily pointed the finger at White male police officers shooting innocent Black men. The confabulation became heated when talking about racism and slavery. Sasha believed that it's easy for Blacks to blame Whites for slavery, for example. This seems to be a common thread that many Blacks want to keep at the forefront when dealing with any race issues of concern today. This makes many Whites feel guilty for an injustice that took place during the slavery years (1619-1865) in America.

Sasha suggested to her nephew and brother-in-law that the majority of Blacks only want to discuss slavery and racism as it is documented in American History. No one wants to think about the slavery of Blacks among Blacks in Africa during the colonial period when European slave merchants purchased them from Black slave merchants on the western coast of Africa. The French, English, Portuguese, Spanish, and others all participated in the slave trade. But, in American History as it is taught in the U.S., the fact that Blacks enslaved Blacks before settling in the U.S. is not discussed. Why would this be important? Well, there is no doubt that Whites inflicted a lot of pain and suffering on Blacks during the era of American slavery, and Whites should be blamed for the atrocities of slavery. But wasn't it also merciless for Black-African tribes to enslave and sell Black Africans to the Europeans back in the 16th and 17th centuries? Why don't Black Americans also want to acknowledge the faults of their forefathers as well? Sasha's brother-in-law retorted emphatically, "But, Sasha, you aren't Black! How would you know how Blacks in America feel today?" Sasha agreed that she wasn't Black, and she couldn't possibly conceive of how it felt to be Black. At the same time, she wasn't going to endorse the guilt of being White as many universities and the American government wanted her, her brother-in-law, nephew, and all Whites to feel. Here lies one reason Americans have trouble discussing race and racism in the United States.

All four friends agreed that slavery and the treatment of Blacks in America should never be forgotten, but at the same time, the discourse should be broader as it includes slavery and race issues from all of its perspectives, as it relates to Blacks, Native Americans, Hispanics, the Irish, and Japanese. Again, when people are forsaken, whether they are Black or White, within their own communities and universities, they adhere and defend one point of view only. This is a mistake, and this misunderstanding and intolerance are passed on from one generation to another. It becomes ingrained in their persona and cultural makeup. As a result, it becomes a topic that is not examined, and because of this, more conflicts and divisions ensue. This leads to more violence and hatred among ethnic groups not only in America but in the rest of the world as well. This is the main reason why we as humans are "jars of clay" that must be shaped across all races. It must be an all-inclusive dialogue among people of divergent ethnic groups that must take place globally with the inclusion of objective as well as subjective points of view when disputing and debating slavery.

This type of heated exchange had a long way of evolving before it could ever take place. People were not culturally and morally mature enough to participate in this kind of verbal back-n-forth according to Rafael. He often wondered where this inability to explore issues came from. In many affluent neighborhoods across America, people don't talk to one another. In Rafael's neighborhood in Alamo Heights, Texas, neighbors don't even look at one another when they are outside raking leaves or just picking up the morning newspaper. Are we that busy where we can't take the time to greet one another? To ask a simple question, "How are you today?" One of Rafael's neighbor, Estela, seems to remain in her house alone most of the day. About twice a year, he runs into her outside watering the grass during the sweltering months of summer. If he does not say, "hola," she does not raise her eyes to greet him. Rafael always initiates the give-n-take, and they usually have a warm colloquy about family and trips taken. But it's sad to think Estela would continue tending to her yard without acknowledging Rafael if he never initiated the "symposium." What is wrong with this picture?

Sasha concurred with Rafael's observations about our neighborhoods in America. So, if this is a microcosm of how we interact in our communities across America, how are we equipped to debate and liaise internationally with others? This, according to Sasha, was the real downfall of the 21st century. With all of the technology available to us today, we are incapable of communicating in the same language with one another. As she reminisced about an interview she saw last night with her husband, Ismael, on *Super Soul Sunday* with Oprah Winfrey conversing with the former first lady, Michelle Obama, she thought about their exchange of ideas. In her book, *Becoming Michelle Obama*, Mrs. Obama discusses her upbringing in Chicago in a barrio integrated in the 1980s when she was in the first grade but became almost completely inhabited by African Americans by the time she was in the eighth grade. Anglos were exiting the vicinity as Blacks moved there. She remembers seeing her father go to work every day in his shipyard uniform and her mother working as a school teacher. She and her brother were about the same age, and their aunts, uncles, and grandparents all lived nearby. Michelle went on to Princeton and then to Harvard where she received a law degree. She worked hard and overcame the barriers created by racism, excluding Blacks from the same economic, social, and educational opportunities afforded to Anglos. She later met and married Barack Obama, the first African-American president ever elected in the United States. They both overcame the injustices of racism to rise above and succeed.

The question Sasha meditated on was: Isn't Michelle Obama contributing to the horrible divide of present-day racism as she shares her story? There is no doubt she surmounted many limitations as an African-American woman who grew up poor and saw her parents struggle to survive economically. But she did have the "juncture" to better herself, and would this have been possible in any other country other than the United States with all of its imperfections? Sasha was sure Mrs. Obama was grateful for everything she achieved as an American, but it seems like this could have been stressed more. Would she and her husband have experienced the same success in France or Germany, for example, where there has never been a Black president elected? This is the great contradiction of the United States. It is a country that is still healing from slavery, a Civil War, and the civil rights movement of the 1960s. Nevertheless, America has come a long way in improving race relations, and Mrs. Obama did express her optimism for the future.

What interested Sasha was that racism and its divisions should not just be pitted, primarily, between Whites and Blacks because there is an apparent schism among members of the same Anglo and African-American communities. Racism also subsists among Republicans and Democrats, regardless of their ethnic makeup. Sasha believed this is what Mrs. Obama failed to mention and observe in her memoir. We as a nation have to evolve beyond this label of "racism" that we continue to perpetuate in our political and social climate. This was the real paradigm that should be addressed, and Sasha believed that a third political party needed to evolve from the destruction and ashes that the Republicans and Democrats continue to fuel with their animosity towards one another and the American people.

KAYAKING

IT WAS MONDAY, the 26th of November, and the weather was picture perfect with a clear blue sky and half-denuded trees. Leaves laid everywhere in a crisp air of 58 degrees with a high of 64. Rafael decided to take advantage of his day off since working part-time as an interpreter in San Antonio. He loaded up his truck with a bright yellow Tsunami 140 kayak and drove up the road to Rio Vista Park in San Marcos, Texas, about an hour drive. There he parked by the park ranger's office near the waterfalls. He ate his peanut butter and jelly sandwich as he prepared himself for about a 15.5-mile trek down the San Marcos River to Staples Dam. The green water was glistening as he covered his face, arms, and legs with sunscreen. He wore a black Under Armour beanie with a black wide brimmed hat with a cover for his neck along with dark sunglasses sustained around his neck with an adjustable cord. Nervously, he climbed into his kayak after calling his wife, Josefina, to let her know he was beginning. This was the longest distance he ever kayaked, so his goal was to finish his journey before dusk. It was approximately 1:30 in the afternoon. He crossed the river immediately to portage since he wasn't experienced enough to ride down the two small waterfalls at the beginning of the course. He reentered the river next to the second waterfall. The water was flowing nicely as his Werner carbon fiber paddles engaged the water.

He soon disappeared into the green vegetation hovering over the river. After a few turns, he was floating under the IH-35 highway. Here he was on a Monday on a river while most people were working.

It was a reminiscent time as the water flooded his mind with memories of living and going to school at Southwest Texas State University in San Marcos. He remembered so clearly running through the same underpass he was now crossing with his friend, Daniel. The many times they ran past Cuevas Produce on River Road. A new conglomerate of condominiums aligned the right-hand side of this once dense bountifully green road. About a mile down, they would run down Old Martindale Road, which was still the same. It was filled with trees, and the two ranch houses at the first corner looked the same. The road eventually dipped down towards a bridge crossing the Blanco River, which fed into the San Marcos River. The 10 foot dirt embankments were still present along with the array of rocks soaking in the trickling water and sunshine. There was a slight hill past the bridge with a cattle ranch on the left-hand side. It was commonplace to hear the rustling sounds of the longhorns in the corral.

Little did we know this was where they were loaded up onto trailers as they were transported to the slaughter house. Cowhands lived adjacent to the "stockade" in trailer homes, which hadn't changed in more than 20 years. We carved that road with our footsteps like water leaving its imprint on the rocks. Memories filled the falling leaves as Rafael drove down this road earlier and as he would drive down this bypass later to pick up his kayak in Staples.

After immersing himself in the porous and wet stream just beyond the Rio Vista Dam, he floated to the right under another bridge as he approached another *petite* embankment, which was difficult to discern its depth and level of risk. Rafael continued on to the left avoiding the flow pulling his kayak towards the waterfall. He could now see that it was too treacherous to navigate down the levee. He proceeded to cross over to the right side to find a good location to portage, but the area was fenced in. As he proceeded to cross to the other side where there was a large rock, the water sucked him into the current leading to the dam. Fortunately, his stern was caught on a rock barely keeping him from moving forward over the dam. As he tried to back paddle to move his boat, he was unable to budge from his location. His only option was to exit the cockpit of the kayak, which took some balancing to accomplish. Once he was out, he was able to step onto some *piedras* (stones) in shallow water, but when he took another step, it was too deep. Rafael began to breaststroke with his left hand, leaving his right hand clutched to the kayak with his paddle securely attached to the boat with its crisscrossing cords. His legs were a little heavy due to the Keen sandals he was wearing. Luckily, he was able to move backwards away from the current pulling him into the dam. He proceeded to the large "cabochon" rock where he was able to portage. His fanny pack was full of water, but his cellphone was dry since he had packed it in two Ziploc bags. Some water had also entered the compartments of his kayak where his lunch box was full of water. He drained the water from his soaked food receptacle, and he also overturned his kayak to remove the excess water.

After regaining his composure and thoughts, he reentered the water. He saw what appeared to be a family of turtles sunbathing on a large stump jetting out from the water. There were two large ones, the mother and father, along with two smaller ones lined up evenly. They seemed to smile and remained motionless as I passed nearby. On the other side of the bank, a beautiful blue heron stretched its wings as it took flight in slow motion, balancing itself with its large beak. It was a prehistoric scene, one he recalled seeing in a dinosaur book as a child.

As he fast-forwarded to Saturday, after traversing the river on Monday, Rafael prepared himself for the race. He unloaded his kayak at the Rio Vista Park in front of the waterfalls. It was a crisp morning with sun bathing the early morning with its refreshing scent. It was cloudless with an easy wind moving the restful leaves in the trees. Other participants assembled as we placed our boats on the grass just above the waterfront.

Rafael placed his 12-foot black cable and lock in the back hatch of the stern along with an extra water bottle in case he capsized and lost the bottle positioned in front of his seat. He also fastened his red life vest on the cords in back of his seat. After placing his kayak on the grass with his carbon fiber paddle and cycling gloves to keep his hands from blistering, he returned to his white Toyota truck to begin the ritual of applying sunscreen to his face, his arms, and exposed legs. He also silenced his cell phone and placed it into two sealed-tight Ziploc bags and placed it in his black fanny pack with a power bar, spare key, and small pocketknife. There was no reason to bring the knife other than to leave it in the fanny pack where he kept it stored.

After this ritual, he wrapped a bandanna around his neck, and adjusted some disposable sunglasses with a sustaining strap around his neck. He placed a black Under Armour beanie on his head, making sure it did not cover his ears due to the pressure it would place on his sunglasses, which would cause a headache. On top of the skullcap, he wore a black wide-brimmed hat with a flap in the back to protect his neck from the sun. Rafael was concerned about sun exposure since he spent a lot of time outdoors. It was about twenty till ten when he lowered his boat into the river. He started at 10 a.m. sharp with the other recreational kayaks while the faster carbon fiber and Kevlar boats started intermittently about 40 to 45 minutes later. There were a total of about 25 competitors. Rafael knew that he wouldn't be one of the top finishers, like he was accustomed to in triathlons, so he reminded himself of this. But this didn't mean that he wouldn't try. The event would be like the scene he viewed on Monday morning, two days after the race, when he was composing this experience on his computer in the clear and beautiful yellow dining room in San Antonio. Two squirrels circled the huge pecan tree in front of him. He looked through a window directly in front of him where the diamond-shaped frame enclosed a snapshot of the cavernous trunk where it bifurcated into a V-designed abstraction. There stood one squirrel as the other settled on the right side of the bark, both resting and twitching as they waited for the next move the other would make.

Shortly after the race began and Rafael portaged around the first small waterfalls, two boats in front of him reentered the water. After circling down the river for about ten minutes and floating under two bridges, he approached one participant and tried to paddle past him in an open area, which quickly turned into a narrow passage on the right. The path became treacherous due to a web of vines reaching out from a tree. As Rafael proceeded to pass, his boat floated into the vines and he tried to duck to protect his head. Unexpectedly, one of the vines wrapped around his neck forcing him to turn, which caused his boat to turn slowly to the left and capsize. The water was about ten feet deep, and his head was completely submersed in the water. It was a frightening moment as he struggled to hold on to his boat and paddle and, more importantly, to gasp for a breath of air. Fortunately, he recovered after arriving to an embankment where he could stand on ground and turn over his boat to empty the water. He capsized one more time on his trek down the river, and after he recovered he realized his stern was sinking. Somehow he had punctured a hole in the back of his kayak, and water was filling up in his back hatch. Rafael believed the puncture occurred when he was portaging his boat at Martindale Dam. He had to drag his kayak down some steep rocks, causing the stern to slam onto the hard granite from a three-foot drop as he approached the water's edge to reenter. At the time, he didn't know he had a hole, but as he paddled with about two miles to the finish, he noticed water filling up behind his seat. Plus, the kayak was tilting to the left, and it was more difficult to gain speed.

As he shared his story with Josefina later in the evening, he was glad he did the race. As Jeff, one of the paddlers, said: "It's inevitable to not run into problems kayaking down the river. What's important is not to panic and solve the "existential obstacles" as quickly as possible. Paddling is much like life in which issues will surface." Overall, the river was an idyllic setting with its dense vegetation, large cypress trees, families of turtles, blue herons, and an occasional "devilish cottonmouth Texas snake" with inflated lungs dancing and frolicking daringly nearby atop the clear greenish water of the river's sea with the sun gleaming through its porous glass. He knew he would train a little more if he attempted to participate in this event next year. Since he had not been running for the past four months due to inflammation and a frayed Achilles tendon, this was a great activity and exercise to do while he recovered.

PERSPECTIVES

THE FOLLOWING DAY Josefina and Rafael read about the passing of the 41st president, George H. W. Bush, who was 94 years old. They were touched by a picture of Sully, his yellow Labrador service dog, laying by his casket, which was draped by the American flag. He was a great president who confronted Saddam Hussein and his aggression during the Gulf War of 1991, and Bush also laid the ground work for signing the nuclear disarmament with Mikhail Gorbachev and the Soviet Union. He led with a genteel "noblesse oblige" in contrast with the foulmouthed confrontational approach of President Donald Trump. Bush was known for his ability as a Republican to decree beyond the aisle to reach agreements whereas as Trump has driven a wedge between both parties and the American people.

As a result, our nation is more divided than ever before. But, in a way, this may be part of a purging process that must take place in the United States. It may be time for a third party to evolve to challenge the status quo of the Democratic and Republican Parties.

The following night Josefina and Rafael discussed a trip for the following year to Croatia and Serbia. They were planning to do a bike ride vacation along the Alps and seaboard of these countries. They would bike for seven days with the touring company Backroads that would transport their luggage from one destination to the other. This would be ideal since Rafael had not been able to run on his right Achilles tendon, which he had been resting now for about four months. Normally, Rafael would run on their yearly vacations since he was an avid athlete who enjoyed training on a regular basis. For this trip, all the hotels would be booked for each night, and most of the meals would be planned for them. The distances covered each day would range from 20 to 60 miles. Plus, there would be a sag wagon that would pick up any rider who wasn't able to complete any given planned "stretch" for the day. This comforted Josefina since she did not ride as much as Rafael. She was a good athlete at the ripe age of 62, but she preferred to play tennis as her main form of exercise.

The trip would give them an opportunity to learn about Croatia and Serbia, and they would also be able to experience the stunning and delightful landscapes of these countries.

They both enjoyed travelling, and one of their goals was to visit a different country each year. Even though they didn't speak the languages of all cultures, it would allow them to discover a new world. It would also be exciting to taste their native food. As they both aged, they realized the significance of taking advantage of these "opportune junctures" since there would come a time when it would be a more formidable challenge to *faire du voyage* and see foreign places. Rafael often compared his wanderlust need to frequently go on a trek to his athletic pursuits. The fire inside for these pursuits did not burn quite as intensely as they used to, but he realized this was part of life. He discerned he had reached many of his peak performances as an athlete; many times now, at the age of 60, he needed to embrace the joy again of exercising and training. He reflected on a quote from an 85-year-old athlete running the San Antonio Marathon this past weekend who stated in the *San Antonio Express-News:* "I no longer am concerned about competition or leisurely hobby. I just like immersing myself in a place of silence as I "frolic" and struggle with the course." That's all we can really do, and it's a great testament to living to be able to return to the essence of any athletic competition.

The fall rain descended on Rafael's home in San Antonio as he was writing and taking time to meditate on life. It was a quiet "longer space" as he juggled his "figurative pins" of being semiretired and having the house to himself in the early morning. Josefina was still working as an endocrinologist, and she would leave promptly for work every morning by 7 a.m. with Thursdays being the exception. She looked beautiful as she would leave every morning with that ephemeral smile that emanated from her angelic persona. At times it was difficult to organize his time since there was no pressure to complete any given activity at any specific deadline. It seemed like often his days would be consumed with swimming, biking, and lifting weights on alternate days. Most weeks, he would also make a regular trip to the grocery store to buy groceries and to fill a vase at home with another bouquet of colorful tulips or antique roses for Josefina. Certain routines were entrenched in his daily existence.

Today Rafael rode his blue and gray trek mountain bike down Salado Creek for about 34 miles. It was a nice leisurely ride since he was recovering from a strong ride two days ago on his trek Y-Foil vintage road bike. He rode 60 miles and averaged 19.2 mph. It was a good effort, and there was relatively little wind. Yesterday he swam about 2,000 yards and lifted weights at the gym. So, today he basically did a recovery ride. As he rode, he was pondering whether to continue studying to become certified as a court interpreter. He had already taken the written exam, which he passed on two occasions. However, he failed the oral exam at least three times. He studied and prepared himself somewhat by practicing the three modes, which were sight translation, consecutive, and simultaneous. For the sight translation portion, he had to read a one-page legal document written in English and interpret it into Spanish; then, he read a document in Spanish and interpreted it into English.

The consecutive mode involved deciphering questions and answers from a deposition in both Spanish and English. When the lawyer asked the client a question in English, it had to be explicated exactly into Spanish. When the client responded in Spanish, the response had to be interpreted in English. Interpreters had to develop a good memory, and they also had to master a fast technique for note-taking to remember details, dates, and times. The simultaneous mode was challenging because the interpreter had to vociferate the exact words of a judge or lawyer from English to Spanish as he/she was speaking.

Rafael contemplated the long investment required to become certified as a court interpreter. It would require a lot of studying, and he was ambivalent as to whether he wanted to dedicate that much time and effort.

Furthermore, if he were to become certified, did he really want to spend a lot of time in court working? It seemed like court interpreting would be a lot more time-consuming than the jobs he was doing now interpreting for schools and hospitals. Most appointments with doctors and patients or school officials and parents, whose child might be receiving special education services, were limited to one hour or an hour and a half at most. He was getting used to working less so that he had time to train and write. Nevertheless, he struggled with whether to continue studying to try to pass the oral exam or not.

At a recent job at the San Antonio Municipal Court on Frio Street downtown this past week, he reflected about meeting with a woman judge, named the Honorable Rosa Zarzamora, and Mr. Mora. The prosecutor, Mr. Smiley, was also present. Mr. Smiley told Rafael that they were waiting on the arrival of the police officer involved in the incident with Mr. Mora. I learned as we waited that Mr. Mora was stopped in his vehicle for drunk driving; however, he indicated that he wasn't drinking but just tired from working all day. As Rafael listened to him speak in Spanish, he was difficult to understand because he talked softly and stuttered every so often. Mr. Mora evidently had other encounters with the law, and he stated that it was common for officers not to show up to court on the first appearance. This was aggravating because he had to waste time getting off from work to come to this court hearing whereas it was customary for officers to skip the initial appearance. Judge Zarzamora asked Mr. Mora if he agreed to reset the trial for another date. She indicated that if the officer did not show up for the next trial date, the case would be dismissed. Mr. Mora expressed his displeasure with the law explaining that police officers and courts can do whatever they want to criminalize innocent people. Reluctantly, Mr. Mora accepted the new trial date. Rafael was able to interpret in the municipal court even though he was not state certified as an interpreter. If it were a criminal court, he would not be allowed to interpret without the proper credentials.

From personal experience, Rafael was able to relate to Mr. Mora's frustration. Rafael had a few incidents in the past with the law, and he felt like many times police officers profile others who may be innocent. But Rafael also knew he was at fault about ten years ago when he was arrested on a harassment charge pertaining to an ex-girlfriend he was dating at the time. He and his girlfriend had broken up, and he left some unpleasant messages in her voice mail, which she recorded and provided in a police report. There were also inappropriate e-mails they both exchanged with one another. Rafael did not file a police report against her, but she used this evidence in her report in which she felt harassed. At the time, he felt he was being singled out and treated unfairly, but now, he realizes that he was at fault just as much as she was. Nevertheless, she took the right action by filing the report legally. Rafael learned a valuable lesson even though he was angry about it for years afterwards. Later, he was able to see both sides of the story, and he realized after having his hands and feet shackled as he was escorted in a patrol car to jail, that the law enforcement agency was just doing their job. However, it did seem a little excessive to be shackled for such a minor offense. This was humiliating, and it allowed him to empathize with Mr. Mora and others.

There definitely could be more sensitivity between agents of the legal system and their supposed victims. Rafael always found it interesting when he would receive phone calls asking for donations for police officers and their cause. What irritated him was the aggressive way they asked for donations? They wanted you to commit to giving a dollar amount immediately, and if not, they rudely would hang up the phone. In a small way, this reflected how many in society view the police and officers of the law. There needs to be more pleasantries exchanged between officers and those they encounter. Rafael believed that officers, for example, could be friendlier when they are at restaurants eating during their shifts. Maybe they could greet other patrons of the eatery with kind words. It just seemed like there are not many interactions between police officers and others in society unless there was an offense that had been committed. Maybe this offense was the result of a miscommunication or misunderstanding. In our society, if neighbors don't even communicate, then why would police officers want to greet others? This is a major societal problem.

NEW ORLEANS AND FAMILY

I T'S DECEMBER 26TH, and Rafael was drinking a tall latte at the corner of Magazine and Washington Streets in New Orleans. He had just finished swimming at the YMCA on Oretha St. about an hour ago. He had dropped Josefina off at the Commander's Palace Restaurant where she met up with her good friends from high school, Karla and Brianna. They had a tradition of meeting every Christmas if they were all in the Big Easy. It was a mild day, and Starbucks was not too busy. The fresh cup of coffee allowed him to reflect on the year behind him and the year to come. He remained in the present as he observed the dark-stained wooden table where he was sitting, which was accompanied by four chairs of a similar hue. He thought about his frayed right Achilles tendon as a runner passed by. It had been five months since he had been able to run. He was blessed he could still swim and ride his bike. Josefina was very understanding and flexible by allowing him time to train and exercise.

He pondered the Christmas meal at Karolina and Jorge's home in Pearl River yesterday. They shared a sumptuous meal of turkey, ham, green bean casserole, broccoli salad, sweet potato puree, macaroni & cheese, and some hot biscuits with a creole dish consisting of shrimp and squash. The conversation was light touching on politics, but not delving deep into the issues. Beto, one of Josefina's cousins, joked about someone in the family going on a date with a Black-American man. Most everyone laughed. Another comment was made about a friend of the family donating money to a Black cause, which gave that person a right to comment on issues affecting Black lives. Another burst of laughter erupted. Rafael did not cachinnate since he found the jokes offense and racist. It seems like it was prevalent among many families to make racist jokes as if that were entertaining. The irrelevance of many conversations among family members often seemed meaningless and superficial. Most colloquies fade after the first inquiry is asked. The ability or willingness of people to ask questions is a lost art. People are either not interested in what others have to say, or they just lack any intellectual curiosity.

The espresso machine whirled in the background as Rafael thought about the theme of this book *A Jar of Clay*. There is no such thing as a "finished jar of clay" since life continues to evolve and recreate itself. Most of us wake up with the need to work to earn a salary to pay for our homes and necessities. Whether we go to college or not, we are faced with the need to work. If we are lucky and save a good portion of our money, we are able to work less, travel more (if we chose to), and reflect on life. Rafael felt like there were a few essentials in his life that he tried to maintain, and these were: exercise, good nutrition, prayer, good sleep, reading, and writing. Although he felt prayer was important, many times he failed at developing his meditative and spiritual life. He read many books on the importance of the breath in calming the mind, and he also knew it was significant to remain in the moment by not allowing the mind to drift into the future or past. This was an exercise that was difficult for him to master. It was demanding for most people, especially Americans, to master since we are preoccupied with work, family, leisure, and the routine of going to church.

The concept of love was a complex one to understand and to exercise. Every religion discussed its value among people of all nationalities and cultures. How do we love ourselves and one another? It's a constant balance we must search for as one considers his/her interests as well as the needs and interests of others. Is this part of the "final word," or is it the elusive word? Love requires man to let go and allow things to be. How do we let go and remain responsible to ourselves and others? Rafael thought of *Nausea*, a novel written by Sartre. Sartre gave life to the things around him: his chair, coffee table, lamp, couch, standing coat hanger, and books. Things take on a personality of their own. Chairs are important because there is a time to sit. Tables are necessary because we need to place our things, like coffee cups, on something to sustain them. Lamps are necessary for reading, cooking, and other activities, especially, at night. We coexist with these things because of their need and codependency between these objects.

What is more introspective than reading and writing? One can spend a lot of time reading the classics, whether it be Shakespeare, Rousseau, Voltaire, John Locke, and others. But of what value are the classics if one does not write his own narrative developing his individual thoughts and philosophy? Most of us live our lives without thinking for ourselves. We watch TV and go to the movies, allowing others to create for us. There is nothing wrong with watching movies, but what Rafael found interesting is that many adults don't create for themselves, whether it be by painting an "abstract mini canvas," writing and singing a song, building something with his own hands, writing a book, or devising a patent for an item to sell. Many of us live our lives completing one task after another. People take trips abroad to taste the food and drink the wine and then tell others about how much they've learned about culture. What is it about culture we should know? Should we attend symphonies by Bach and Wagner across the world and let our friends know how much we appreciate classical music? Should we attend museums with exhibitions of Pablo Picasso, Monet, and Van Gogh to let others know we were there? Maybe these events should teach us the intrinsic value of creating for ourselves. Rafael believed that once this is done, one establishes one's own voice. He remembered as a teacher how he enjoyed creating his own videos for his Spanish classes over the years. The extemporaneous clips were meant to entertain as well as to teach fundamental vocabulary words and grammatical structures from the course curriculum. He integrated many costumes, miniature dolls, and animals in these skits. Students were then required to present their own scripts in groups of two, which incorporated vocabulary and other grammatical structures from the lesson. *Il ne peut pas enseigner* (not teach) directly from the textbook as most language teachers did. They would proceed from one exercise to the next as it was presented in the book. He wanted to generate some unique material, and he encouraged his students to design their own work as well. This is what an education should do and provide for its students.

Josefina and Rafael just returned to San Antonio from a Christmas holiday trip to New Orleans. Josefina grew up in the St. Bernard Parish, just about five miles from the French Quarter and the Café du Monde. They always stayed at Donasio's house on Benjamin Street. It was a two-story home rebuilt after the damage caused to his former home from Hurricane Katrina. Rafael enjoyed watching Josefina interact with her brother. She greeted him the morning after they arrived after driving 10 hours. "How are you, Donasio?" He responded, "Huhh." Donasio had a strong New Orleans's accent. "I'm alrightttt." A few minutes later he was gone on his bike without inviting them to ride. Donasio was a man of few words unless he was talking about the Saints and football or President Trump and how great he was doing. Rafael found Donasio interesting since his persona could be summed up with the expression: "Nola till you die!" This meant that one lived in New Orleans until a person's demise. Josefina loved New Orleans, and Rafael enjoyed watching her relate to and interact with her family and friends who also returned to the city for the Holidays. He relished how she and her family members neglected using past participles correctly in their speech. It wasn't uncommon for them to say, "I have 'went' to a parade downtown." Or, "He have 'ate' the peanuts." There were many linguistic gems to be cherished and enjoyed.

On Christmas Day, Carlos, Josefina's youngest brother who was the fire chief of the station in St. Bernard Parish, joined Donasio, Josefina, and Rafael on a bike ride early after he finished his shift at work. They left Donasio's house at about 7:45 a.m. on their mountain bikes for a ride through the city. They would cross a bridge leading into the Ninth Ward and proceed towards City Park where they would coast on a trail leading to Lake Pontchartrain and old golf courses with interesting and bifurcating paths. It was a tranquil morning with the temperatures in the upper 60s and plenty of sunshine. Josefina truly enjoyed riding with her brothers as they reconnected with one another. The city was dormant this time of the year, which made it that more pleasant riding with reduced vehicular traffic. Old buildings with colorful graffiti interspersed with modern buildings in the new medical center filled the landscape along their ride. Circling through the *senderos* (trails) of the golf course, they rode single file. They enjoyed the ponds hidden in the verdant mixture of mesquite, bamboo, and tall weeds protecting swarms of ducks and the occasional blue herons. They ended up in the French Quarter where they enjoyed hot coffee, almond chocolate croissants, and a spinach quiche at a favorite bakery and eatery.

Biking on Christmas morning, before meeting up with the rest of Josefina's family at Jorge and Karolina's home in Pearl River, had become a tradition for her. Last year she remembered biking with Donasio and Rafael. Donasio donned the same pair of grey shorts with a large hole on the left pant leg with his cycling shorts underneath. He would wear the same outfits for years. The night before he wore an oversized light-blue sweatshirt with large fitting-faded blue jeans to the St. Louis Cathedral for Mass on Christmas Eve. He also sported the same black tennis shoes he had sported for years. Donasio was content with keeping things simple with as little change as possible. He had lived in New Orleans all of his life, and his house was constructed within spitting distance of the plot where the home he grew up in with his six other siblings and parents had been built. This *hogar* (home) as well was destroyed by Hurricane Katrina. Donasio's curiosity of the world did not extend beyond New Orleans. Rafael found this amazing and in sharp contrast to Josefina who had travelled the world, studied in several states (Texas, Virginia, and Colorado), and eventually became an endocrinologist. She had a boundless amount of energy and curiosity much like her late mother Joanna who enjoyed and relished immensely nature, travel, and people. There was an infectious aura about Josefina that made her an exceptional woman and human being, which contrasted greatly with Donasio. Interestingly, Donasio was comfortable in his own skin as a single man with no interest in dating women. He was content with hanging out with Carlos and other neighborhood friends. This was evident on game day when Carlos, two of his childhood friends, Jesse (Carlos's stepson), and Donasio ate a muffuletta sandwich before leaving to see a Saints' game at the Mercedes Superdome outfitted in their Saints' t-shirts and caps. Donasio took his sweet tea with him as the others prepared to drink beer and cheer on their favorite team. Merl, one of Carlos's friends and coworker at the fire station, already had a Bud Light in hand.

MEXICAN AMERICAN AND POLITICS

RAFAEL HAD MANY ruminations in his mind as he and Josefina returned to San Antonio after their lovely Christmas break in New Orleans. Josefina was off a whole week from work. As Rafael perused the *San Antonio Express-News* the following morning with his coffee and foamed half-and-half cream, he read an article in which Julián Castro, the former mayor of San Antonio, declared to run as Democratic presidential candidate for the next elections. What was interesting was that he considered himself a Latino because he is Hispanic and grew up in the iconic West Side of San Antonio. However, Rafael thought it was a paradox since he did not speak Spanish.

He declared himself as a candidate at the Guadalupe Theatre, which is located in the center of West Side. The West Side is predominately a poor and Hispanic neighborhood in San Antonio. Our Lady of the Lake University and the Basilica of la Virgen de Guadalupe are located within this community. Rafael wondered to himself about the false pretense of calling himself a Latino and valuing the Mexican-American culture. That's kind of like an Anglo, being born and raised in San Antonio, who frequents Mi Tierra Restaurant in the *mercado* downtown and has tried every type of enchilada with mole and tacos; now, he considers himself a

Latino. Octavio Paz, the renowned Mexican writer who wrote *El laberinto de la soledad*, would state that Julián is a *pocho*, a Hispanic who is mestizo but doesn't speak Spanish. If he spoke Spanish, he would be considered lower class because the upper class speaks English to associate more readily with the Anglos by separating themselves from Mexicans or Latinos who only speak Spanish. Furthermore, it is noteworthy to underscore that Mr. Castro is proud because his children are in dual-language programs in school. Is this because he feels guilty for not learning Spanish in high school? Couldn't he begin to learn Spanish now? His mother was a Chicana activist who spoke Spanish, fought for the Chicano cause in the 1960s, and was a founding member of *La Raza Unida*. Mr. Castro is what an avid cyclist would call a *poser*.

Rafael thought about the government shutdown of over a month, which is the longest in U.S. history. President Trump wants Congress to pass a bill for 5.7 billion dollars to fund the wall between Mexico and the U.S. borders along Texas, Arizona, and California. The Democrats are adamant about not funding the wall because they want money appropriated to fund the "Dreamers," those illegal immigrants that have resided in the U.S. already for a long time and for those seeking asylum from their corrupt governments in Guatemala, Honduras, and Mexico. The problem is more complicated than just erecting a wall, but at least a wall would be a deterrent for those seeking to cross illegally. Furthermore, it would assist the Border Patrol Agents in those areas along the border where there is no barrier. Hopefully, then, the U.S. government will look at the other issues that affect immigration, such as government corruption in those Central American and Mexican governments along with the drug epidemic in the U.S. where the primary consumers of cocaine and opioids reside. The gangs in Central America evolved after the guerrilla wars in Honduras, Guatemala, Nicaragua, and El Salvador during the 1970s and 80s. The Partido Revolucionario Institucional (PRI) has dominated the political life of Mexico since the end of the Mexican Revolution in 1921. Drug cartels and bosses like El Chapo Guzmán have dominated the arena by paying off Mexican presidents like Carlos Salinas, Enrique Calderón, and Peña Nieto. American officials need to constantly discuss this corrupt history and present political environment of these countries.

The U.S. must also learn from its mistakes during the Reagan administration which supported and funded the Contras during the Nicaraguan War of the 1980s against the Sandinistas regime, which had defeated President Anastasio Somoza Debayle in July 1979. Mr. Somoza inherited the dictatorship from his elder brother and father ruling Nicaragua for 44 years. The Sandinistas under the leadership of Daniel Ortega imposed many of the hardships and civil rights abuses of the previous dictatorship and now, as president, rules with an iron fist. The U.S. representatives must understand not only the Spanish language but the political histories of these countries to remain in a perpetual dialogue with their corrupt and oppressive governments. This lack of dialogue contributes to the many issues that pertain to immigration and the problems at the U.S. and Mexican border.

Sasha and Rafael would often discuss these issues that neither the Democrats nor Republicans brought to the forefront of their agendas. It's obviously more important than establishing the "wall," a physical barrier between countries. One major problem is the consumption of illicit drugs in the U.S. What are the elements that feed this epidemic? We live in the most prosperous country in the world where unemployment is at an all-time low. The American citizens, for the most part, are materially wealthy but maybe spiritually and intellectually deficient. The difficult issues for Americans are the racial divide between Blacks, Hispanics, and Whites along with other minorities. The division and separation between the rich and poor are problematic. These issues are laborious and arduously painful for Americans to discuss and heal from the brutal Civil War where these conflicts were at the frontline, especially the horrific period of slavery. In a way, the U.S. continues to be enslaved by its inability to dialogue. Schools, universities, and public government institutions have become "vehicles" for driving individuals to obtain degrees and licensures to enrich and feed the capitalistic appetite. The *apetito* is never satiated because the hunger for more continues to grow.

Today, on January 21, 2019, we celebrate the life of the late Martin Luther King Jr. who had a *Rêve* (dream) of a united people in the U.S. He dreamed (*Soñó*) of schools that were entirely integrated with Black, White, Hispanic, and children of all ethnic backgrounds learning and growing together. He dreamed of a society (*Sociedad*) with equal opportunities for all people, and where *toda la gente* (persons) would be treated with respect, honor, and dignity. We have come a long way, but we still have an endless trail to traverse as evidenced in the constant clash between police officers and young Black men. It is also evident that most penitentiaries in this country are filled primarily with Black and Hispanic inmates. There is a societal epidemic we constantly need to address. Rafael remembers reading about the ideas of Ayn Rand in which she discusses these "coteries" formed in our society. Not only are there clans among families where members are staged against each other, but there are societal-communal "insiders" where ethnic groups are encouraged to dislike one another. It is human nature to protect and preserve one's "racial stock." As this discussion about the many affairs of their "cultural communities" and the world continued to intrigue Rafael, Josefina, Sasha, and their friends, they often asked themselves the question: "What is the final word on these matters?" "Is there such a thing?"

Is it possible there is no final word? The answer is found in the collection of words that stem from a perpetual dialogue. Rafael believed the conversation must include all areas of the human condition. As he contemplated the reaction to the article *"El señor Castro no habla español,"* which he wrote for the *San Antonio Express-News*, he recalled someone stated that many Mexican Americans were punished and reprimanded for speaking Spanish in schools during the 1950s and 60s in the United States. Many were told to go back to Mexico for speaking Spanish, and many were and are denied jobs today *por hablar* their native language. There is some certainty to this claim today even though it is not as pronounced. Many Mexican Americans who choose not to identify with Hispanics by learning Spanish should just consider themselves Americans and not Mexican Americans. Rafael thought they should value their Mexican ancestry by learning *su lengua native* (native language) just as they esteem their American birth by learning English. Many Mexican Americans struggle with their identity because they succumb to the pressure of assimilating to the American culture. There is nothing wrong with integrating from the standpoint of becoming fluent in English and accepting the human rights of the Constitution. However, one should not be influenced by a small portion of American society that would disapprove of speaking other languages like Spanish fluently.

When Julián Castro announced his candidacy to run for presidency for the 2020 election in the iconic West Side of San Antonio where he grew up, maybe he should have conceded he doesn't feel the need to learn Spanish. But he should not pretend to be a true Latino, one who speaks both languages fluently. On the other hand, he should concede he is a monolingual Mexican American who is a fluent English speaker *solamente*.

Julián y Joaquín Castro, political Democratic twins—*Pochos Con Caras De Nopal* from San Antonio, Texas, are U.S citizens of Mexican origin who DO NOT Speak a LICK of Spanish; this is why they are RACISTS IMPOSTERS of the Liberal, Socialist and DEMOCRATIC Latino, Hispanic, and Mexican American vote—those who don't speak Spanish and those who don't speak a lick of Spanish but who speak SPANGLISH; they have no clue of the Mexican traditions or culture—they are RACIST OUTSIDERS pretending to be RACIST INSIDERS. (Julián y Joaquín Castro de San Antonio, Texas son POCHOS, dos gemelos políticos demócratas con CARAS DE NOPAL, que no hablan ni pío de español; por eso, son IMPOSTORES RACISTAS del voto liberal, socialista y DEMOCRÁTA del latino, hispano y mexicoamericano—LOS QUE NO HABLAN Y LOS QUE HABLAN NI PÍO DE ESPAÑOL sino el Spanglish; no tienen ningún conocimiento de las tradiciones y cultura de México—Son RACISTAS DEL GROUP DE AFUERA O "OUTSIDERS" fingiendo ser RACISTAS INTERNOS o RACISTS INSIDERS.)

The Castros and the Socialist Liberal Democratic Party are also racists against Afro Hispanics, African Americans, Asians and all ethnic and racial groups of the world who reside in the United States of America. The U.S. Democrats are representatives and affiliates of "Satan" because they are in favor of maintaining the border open between the U.S. and Mexico to facilitate the sexual trafficking of children from around the world –the worst form of Slavery ever known in the human race and the history of the world—for the very sick pedophiles in the U.S. and throughout the world as this tragedy is well documented and depicted in the movie *Sound of Freedo*m.

Los Castros y el Partido Socialista Liberal Demócrata también son racistas contra los afro hispanos, afronorteamericano, los asiáticos y de todas los grupos étnicos y raciales del mundo que residen en los Estados

Unidos de América. Los demócratas de los Estados Unidos también son representantes y afiliados de Satanás porque están en favor de mantener la frontera abierta entre los Estados Unidos y México para facilitar el tráfico sexual de niños menores—la peor forma de esclavitud que jamás se haya conocido en la historia del mundo—para los enfermos pedófilos de los Estados Unidos de América y del resto del mundo como se señala y resalta en la película *Sound of Freedom*.

POCHOS CON CARAS DE NOPAL is a Mexican idiomatic expression meaning literally, the Castros' mestizo faces, skin color and physical features look like the Mexican Nopal cactus abundant in that country. Figuratively speaking and connotating, they are Mexican Americans who do not speak Spanish, an epidemic in Texas and the U.S. causing RACISM OF THE FIRST DEGREE to flourish against Mexicans, Latinos, Hispanics—and African Americans with their beautiful black skin color regardless of their ability to speak Spanish or not—Latinos who are fluent in Spanish and Mexican Americans who don't *hablar castellano o español*. The Castros, for example, and their associates, *ÓRALE* (all right then, come on) from the West Side of San Anto, say, "Te watcho later" instead of "*Te veo después*", meaning "I will see you later." The Castros are IMPOSTERS of the Liberal Socialist political DEMOCRATIC Biden-Harris-Obama-Ocasio Cortés "CRACKER JACK POLITICAL MACHINE;" thus, tricksters and liars who will say anything to gain the vote and support of the Latinos, Hispanics, and Mexican Americans of Texas and the United States of America.

After reading "What makes a real Latino or American?" in the San Antonio Express News (2/8/19) by Ricardo Pimentel, Rafael would suggest that Tom Brokaw, the veteran journalist, is not an expert on admonishing whether Latinos should assimilate quickly or not into American society. Brokaw also blasted Latinos who are not fluent Spanish speakers. Is Mr. Brokaw fluent in any other language other than English? I would surmise the answer is no; this is seminal to note because he is not able to penetrate the complexities of Hispanic culture from a solely monolingual perspective. In addition, I commend Mr. Pimentel for trying to perfect his Spanish speaking skills by stating, "*Lo siento. Mi español sufre un poco*". (I'm sorry. My Spanish is lacking a bit.)

Does this inability to speak Spanish fluently define Julián Castro, who is running as a Latino presidential candidate, or other Mexican Americans as non-Latinos and non-Americans? No, it does not. However, it puts politicians at a disadvantage because they only represent the English speaking Latinos of our nation. How would Mr. Castro identify with Spanish speaking and bilingual Latinos of the U.S.? Could he also relate and communicate with leaders like Nicolás Maduro, the totalitarian president of Venezuela, for example, in Spanish? Catch phrases like the one Mr. Castro delivered at the 2016 Democratic convention, "¡*Qué Dios los bendiga*!" (God bless you!), would not be sufficient.

Internationally, it would be fundamental to be able to dialogue in Spanish with someone like Maduro and to state: "*El gobierno de los Estados Unidos está en contra de la opresión que impone Ud. sobre su gente*". (The U.S. government is against the oppression you are imposing upon your people.) Of course, they could dialogue in English, but I believe it would be more effective to do so, in this instance, in Spanish. Knowing the political history of a country like Venezuela well and confronting this rogue regime on its human rights violations would be the answer. A relationship could be established by further acknowledging a "*Latinoamérica unida*" (unified Latin America), which was initially espoused by Simón Bolívar, the 19th century revolutionary leader of Venezuela and Colombia.

Furthermore, the observation of whether Joe Biden or Elizabeth Warren are White candidates or candidates who happen to be White is incongruous. Of course, they are White and speak English. But wouldn't it be something if they spoke Spanish fluently? Being bilingual, whether one is Latino or not, would be a wonderful litmus test, the metaphorical image suggested by Mr. Pimentel. In this area Mr. Biden and Mr. Castro are similar because neither one of them are fluent in Spanish; therefore, they can't relate to those bilingual and Spanish speaking Latino Americans and to Spanish and Latin American *políticos*.

It's great that Mr. Castro is a Mexican American who speaks English fluently, but it's unfortunate he was not taught Spanish growing up on the West Side. Generations of Latinos immigrating to the U.S. should assimilate and learn English. This should be encouraged, but a Latino American who does not preserve his native language, in this case Spanish, is contributing to a monolingual America. In my opinion, this would be detrimental to the U.S. in a world that is in need of a "global assimilation." This lack of linguistic inclusion would create a more devastating "cultural wall" than any physical wall that Mr. Castro and others oppose along the Mexican and U.S. border.

This denial of not knowing the Spanish language among Mexican Americans, according to Sasha, is something they want to ignore. Since most Americans are monolingual, they are not able to identify this subtle racism between Mexican Americans who do not embrace and learn Spanish and those that do. In Sasha's mind, Julián Castro and his brother, Joaquín, show favoritism to those Latino Americans who do not speak Spanish; this is a form of bias. It is very unfortunate because Julián is a graduate of Harvard. Knowing he had political aspirations, one would think he would truly value his Hispanic heritage inherited from his grandmother who emigrated from Mexico.

The pressure to remain monolingual is systemic in the United States. As a former Spanish teacher for over 30 years at the junior high, high school, and university levels, Rafael observed firsthand how Americans are failing to learn foreign languages, especially Spanish. It is an embarrassment the average American only knows two incomplete phrases in Spanish: "¿El baño? and "más cerveza, por favor". Utterances for the bathroom and more beer symbolize the nation's intellectual immaturity and naiveté when it pertains to other languages and cultures. Dull curriculums across the American educational spectrum from grade school to universities, like Harvard, focus on the audio-lingual method of teaching foreign languages. This is to say that they have students work through endless exercises in textbooks and lab manuals focusing on rote memorization and endless lectures on grammatical structures. Little time, if any at all, is focused on allowing students to develop their conversational skills with meaningful topics. This methodology would be defined as the Communicative Approach.

CLAY AND LANGUAGES

JOSEFINA AGREED WITH Rafael that *A Jar of Clay* should encompass the significance and desire of a person to become fluent in a second language to better prepare him/her for fostering love not only for oneself, but for others in our own culture and those beyond our familiar borders. This way a deeper compassion for others can be cultivated and nourished. As Josefina thought about this, she recalled the biblical story of the Old Testament in which Jacob received two wives, Leah and Rachel. Leah was the older daughter of Laban. Jacob loved Rachel, the younger daughter, and he agreed to work Laban's land for seven years to earn his right to marry Rachel. After Jacob completed this task, Laban deceived Jacob by offering Leah to him because she was the oldest daughter. According to tradition, the oldest daughter must marry first. Laban told Jacob that he could also marry Rachel later after working for him for another seven years. Jacob obliged by doing so because he truly loved Rachel.

In their many conversations, Sasha could not see the connection between learning another language, love, compassion, and this part of Jacob's story. "How could all of this relate to *A Jar of Clay*, as you've just stated Josefina?" Josefina enjoyed the challenge of making this connection. As she attempted to tie the loose ends together, Jacob learned to love Laban

JAR OF CLAY

and both of his daughters although romantically he loved Rachel the most. He respected Laban's wishes, and he bore four daughters with Leah. Rachel could not bear children, but she had Jacob impregnate her maidservant and claimed the children as her own. Jacob's compassion for all of his family is apparent. Josefina could only imagine this kind of love could only be magnified, first of all by the love Jacob received from the Lord, which is expressed in his love for family. Jacob's love for family is common for many of us today. However, family extends, according to God, to not only our immediate family but to our outer family represented in all the cultures and languages of the world.

Human beings aren't meant to dwell in one family and one culture, which would be defined by Josefina, as the "imprint of clay." If we take Plato's analogy of the prisoners in a cave who are chained so they can only view the wall in front of them, we realize our reality of understanding is limited to things that are closest to us. Behind the men there is a burning fire with puppets walking back and forth in between the fire and the prisoners. They can only see the shadows of objects on the wall; they cannot see the physical objects themselves, like a book or a sword, for example, that the puppets are carrying. As a result, their sense of reality is only formed by what they see and experience. If these prisoners were released from their chains and left the cave, which is the only existence they are familiar with, they would be exposed to a different reality outside of this entrapment. They would see and experience the sun, moon, sky, and many other realities. However, man's interpretation of these circumstances would still be reduced and defined by his senses. The understanding of pure truth could never be grasped by human beings because we are incapacitated, so to speak, by our senses.

By learning a foreign language, according to Josefina, man could expand his ability to experience reality because he leaves his familiar and intimate family or culture to penetrate an unfamiliar environment and tradition. His "imprint of clay" begins to expand into something larger. Not only does he learn the word "book" and "pen," but he also learns *libro* and *pluma*. The clay image in one language expands into a multitude of words in all the languages of the world; therefore, this creates a metonymy in which concepts and ideas continue to evolve with the advances of human thought and discoveries. The impression and final casting become the jar of clay.

This fascinated Rafael as he sipped on his coffee on Tuesday morning in mid-February 2019. He savored the cloudy and cold morning in the sunroom of his home in San Antonio, Texas. He was blessed to sit here quietly surrounded by windows with nature beaming outdoors: the larger than life pecan tree saluting him with its irregular bark, the swaying leaves of a majestic oak tree in the corner of the backyard, and the Christmas red budding plant to his left. His life was full as he contemplated his upcoming birthday tomorrow, turning 61 years old. He loved his wife Josefina dearly, his parents were still alive and doing well, and his sister, with a lifelong mental illness, lived close by in a home that accommodated her needs as well as those of others. He was able to visit her on a regular basis to walk with her and take her swimming at a local gym. Rafael relished the passage of time as he contemplated *la vida* in its many stages.

VENEZUELA AND SALADO CREEK

RECENTLY, HE WAS concerned about the present situation in Venezuela where Nicolás Maduro ruled with an big stick. Inflation was sky high, and the people were suffering from high unemployment and a scarcity of food. Mr. Juan Guaidó was popular among the people, and the majority wanted Maduro to resign. The U.S. and the international community were pressuring Maduro to turn over the regime to Guaidó. Many countries sent humanitarian aid (medical supplies and food), which Maduro did not allow to be distributed in his country. He claimed his countrymen and state would not tolerate outside interference in Venezuelan matters since they would be handled internally. As a result, the aid was sitting at a checkpoint on the border of Colombia and Venezuela while thousands of Venezuelans fled the country to neighboring countries. This type of totalitarian regime represented a common trend that affected many Latin American countries after World War II. Venezuela and Cuba were probably the only two countries that hung on to this dictatorial past. The need to control and rig the elections were characteristics of this oppressive style of government. With the lack of diversification and foreign investment, these countries were subject to poverty and increased instability.

The leftist writer, Noam Chomsky, would blame the United States for its imperialistic imprint and involvement in the affairs of many Central and Latin American countries during the past century. However, Chomsky would not address the human rights violations of dictators like Pinochet in Chile, Trujillo in the Dominican Republic, Somoza in Nicaragua, Castro in Cuba, and the many others. Did these dictators have the right to rule with a big stick and to incarcerate and kill those who opposed them? These dictators controlled the military, which allowed them to enforce their rule of law. The U.S. government may have naively supported some of these totalitarian governments for economic benefit. But the U.S. government did not speak the language of these countries, and they did not truly understand the historical events that shaped these dictatorships. Rafael believed that the elite of these Latin American countries are also to blame because they reaped the monetary and material benefits of these controlling governments. The U.S. and international communities, including France, Spain, Germany, and others, were ineffective in applying the political pressures to force these governments to change.

Traditions and inflexibility are the venomous poisons that allow these regimes to strive. Other examples would include the scandalous sex abuses of the Catholic Church and the Southern Baptists in which the abuse of children was hidden from the public. Catholic bishops and cardinals were reassigned to other parishes after evidence surfaced of their crimes. These abuses were swept under the carpet, and many in the church believed they were above the law. It is only now that Pope Francis held a summit this past weekend (February 23, 2019) to discuss these matters and to implement some changes on how to investigate these incidents more effectively. The result should immediately include a complete inquiry with criminal prosecution and defrocking of those indicted from the church when found guilty. A prison sentence should also be imposed upon the guilty parties. There should be a zero-tolerance policy as instituted in the churches of the United States.

Rafael was enthralled by these issues as he got older. He enjoyed having these exchanges with Josefina, Sasha, and his many friends. On Saturday he and Josefina rode their bikes along Salado Creek near their home in San Antonio. It was here on September 17, 1842 that Colonel Caldwell and Captain John C. Hays with 210 Texan volunteers defeated General Adrián

Woll who commanded 1200 Mexican troops from the Alamo. The Texan army lured the Mexican troops into the embankment of Salado Creek where they were protected by the thicket of trees. This protection allowed them to use their long rifles to inflict damage on the Mexican troops who marched into the ambush with their glistening bayonets and artillery of small cannons. The bloodstained creek kept the secrets of this battle within the pages of its leafed history as it shed its foliage each winter and regained its new verdant cloak each spring. Josefina had not been riding her bike much since she usually preferred to play tennis and swim on the weekends. But this was a moment they could ride together and enjoy the quiet cool February afternoon.

A BICYCLE RIDE AND DEEP THOUGHTFULNESS

THEY ACCESSED THE creek by riding across Austin Highway and Broadway through the Balcones Heights Neighborhood, which led them up a series of steep but short inclines warming their leg muscles quickly. Josefina had just purchased a wider bicycle seat, which provided more comfort and less distress on her butt. From there, they traversed Wurzbach Rd. and crossed Eisenhower Bridge before settling onto the Salado Creek Greenway Trail. They initially crossed a small bridge at the beginning of the runnel. The wind blew softly as they traversed the tree-lined path, and the late afternoon sun filtered gently through the leaves and branches.

Josefina rode methodically at her easy pace, and Rafael stayed ahead of her for part of the way. He would frequently turn around and allow her to catch up with him. He would banter with her saying, "Go baby, go. And, look at Pachi... You look precious." Pachi was a nickname he created for her years ago. It was short for *Mapache*, which means raccoon in Spanish. Many years ago while still in bed, Josefina rose quickly from sleeping and opened the shutter and window of their bedroom because she heard something rustling outside. To her surprise there was a raccoon that had lifted the black rat poison dispenser and was shaking it to get to the goodies inside. Josefina yelled, "Stop that. Put that down and go away." The raccoon was startled, just as much as I was, threw the dispenser in the air, and fled away. Then, she closed the window and shutter and came back to bed. Rafael thought this was totally hilarious as he was awoken from his deep sleep. As a result, the nickname stuck because it was part of Josefina's personality to constantly do 20 or more tasks at the same time, constantly going and doing things like a *mapache*. According to Rafael's standards, Josefina was truly *preciosa*.

Rafael found himself returning to *Going Home* by Thich Nhat Hanh, the Buddhist thinker and monk. Rafael was pondering the practice of blissful consciousness as Nhat Hanh describes in his book. He states that during walking meditation one becomes "solicitously zealous and conscious" and aware of every step one takes. We, as individuals, have the ability to cultivate the inner abstract "stillness" of thoughts every minute of every day. It is not a notion but a powerful source of energy that comes from within. At Plum Creek, a Buddhist village outside of Bordeaux, France, where Hanh lives and conducts workshops, there is a saying that insightful *Ensimismamiento* (mindful turning within self) is the Buddha. He states that Buddha can also be God. *Dios* is not a notion but a real being. God lives within us; if we access God, we can receive his energy. This energy is the solid base that sustains us. It is a state of "reverent ruminating pensiveness," concentration, and wisdom that can protect us. It provides a path for us to take. If we follow this direction, we are happy. If we don't, we are lost and unhappy, a state of Dantesque inferno.

Josefina reminded Rafael of the invaluable significant "paramountcy" of giving all things to God. When "existential and non-existential chattels," good and bad, are given to the Holy Spirit, which comes from God, we become enlightened. Rafael struggled with this some this past year since he was not able to run due to a frayed Achilles tendon in his right foot. Although he had not run for approximate seven months, she intently "bethought" compassionately to him that it will get better and to give it to God. It was hard for the negativity to seep into his consciousness since he felt like he was doing the right things by icing, stretching, and applying electromagnetic heat to the affected area. He was delightfully joyful and appreciatively obliged he could still bike and swim. But Josefina was right. Rafael needed to practice the inner abstract "quietness" of thoughts every day to replace the negativity with Gods' peace and divine assurance. This insightfulness from within reminds an individual there will always be a battle between deep thoughtfulness and a wondering mind.

RAFAEL AND JOSEFINA enjoyed drinking coffee with frothed half-and-half on weekend mornings as they perused the *San Antonio Express-News* and the article The U.S. Border and Extortion and bribery in Mexico and Central America at their mahogany-colored dining room table. They often discussed the insidious back and forth among politicians concerning the wall along the border. Rafael crafted his own opinion on this topic for the editorial section of the newspaper. According to him, American politicians waste time debating whether to build or not to build the wall along the U.S. and Mexican dividing parameter. Illegal immigration to the U.S. from Central America and Mexico will continue because of the rampant profligacy in these countries among all branches of government, the judicial, and police systems. *La mordida* (the bribe) is part of the cultural makeup of these countries. A basic traffic violation, for example, can be avoided by paying a police officer a *mordida* so that a ticket is not issued. While there are innumerable cases of extreme malfeasance in these countries, there are a few in Mexico that readily come to mind.

Extreme malfeasance in Mexico dates back to Hernán Cortés, the Spanish conquistador who sailed to Veracruz, Mexico in 1521 with approximately 500 Spaniards. This event initiated the Conquest of Mexico and the rest of Latin America by Spain. The Spaniards (*peninsulares*) came with the sole purpose of stealing gold and land from the Aztecs. The *peninsulares* established themselves much like the Mafia did by selling government posts and land among themselves. In 1876 Porfirio Díaz ruled as a ruthless dictator until the Mexican Revolution of 1910-21. The Indigenous and mestizo population were second-class citizens then and remain so today.

Not much has changed in the 21st century. Enrique Peña Nieto, the former president of Mexico (2012-2018), and the First Lady built a $7 million mansion with government funds funneled to their personal bank accounts. They named it *la Casa Blanca* (the white house). Another former Mexican president, Carlos Salinas de Gortari (1988-1994), fled his country after the devaluation of the *peso*, the worst economic crisis to date. His brother, Raúl, who worked for the government, stashed $83.9 million in

Swiss bank accounts. It was believed to be acquired from laundering drug trafficking money. This type of extravagance is common among the elite, which forms 10% of the population while 30% are middle class and 60% live in poverty.

Furthermore, it is known that former Mexican governors like Humberto Moreira of Coahuila and Tomás Yarrington of Tamaulipas invested ill-gotten money in the U.S. with impunity. The U.S. Department of State and Justice Department have not taken a hard stance on extortion and bribery and on how the American financial system facilitates it, according to Tony Payán in his article "Why the U.S. needs to help Mexico fight corruption." Much like the conquistadores who fled back to Spain with galleons full of gold, many current politicians and their families depart their country with stolen goods.

Jorge Ramos, a news anchor for Univisión, proposes to combat profligacy by creating an International Commission Against Corruption (ICAC) in Mexico under the auspices of the United Nations. This was done in Guatemala in 2007, and it was successful in removing President Otto Pérez Molina and his vice president, Roxana Baldetti, from office. If Mexican presidential candidates would agree to such a delegation, it would be a twofold approach for combating corruption from the inside-in and the outside-in. The commission would operate under Mexican law as it conducted criminal investigations and proposed reforms to the judiciary. However, many Mexican politicians would oppose this because the low-life Gucci degenerate system preserves their status.

The U.S. government from both parties should support this type of approach. Proficiency in Spanish and knowledge of Mexican history and politics would aid American diplomats and politicians tremendously.

The endless debate about the wall, whether it should be erected or not, is like placing a Band-Aid over the cancerous-exploited demoralization. Josefina was befuddled as to why politicians and other governmental officials do not keep this common knowledge of infantile jobbery at the forefront of discussions of this type. Rafael believed that a massive bulwark could help the Border Patrol in reducing the number of illegal immigrants entering the U.S., but it should be implemented with anti-corruption policies addressing the inherent failures and corrosive nature of the political "immature-unimpressive-oppressive" blueprints in Mexico as well as in all Central and Latin American countries. Fighting this type of graft and outdated cupidity and debauchery should remain an ongoing priority for all countries to address in a world that is interconnected and depends on the stability of every nation.

Sasha and Marcos met up with Rafael last Saturday at a local Starbucks on Broadway in San Antonio. Rafael learned that they just returned from a yearlong stay in Honduras. Sasha and Marcos were dismayed when they read Rubén Navarrette's article "U.S. identity crisis behind border hysteria," published on March 12, 2019 in the *San Antonio Express-News*. They thought it was interesting how both political parties and American journalists were intent on stating that many feared the "browning" of America. The common denominator in America is to want to dwell on the racial divide, in this case, pitting Whites against Latinos.

After travelling for many years and speaking Spanish to many people in Mexico and other countries throughout Central and Latin America, Marcos believed most immigrate because of the endless and ceaseless graft at all levels of government that keeps them unemployed and uneducated. The majority prefer to remain in their countries if they were not riddled with crime and economic instability. By understanding the historical background of Guatemala, for example, it becomes evident as to why it is and remains a breeding ground for the pestilent carrion of greed by the cowardly-dishonorable-powerful classes of the elite and Catholic Church.

Pedro Alvarado, a Spanish conquistador, conquered Guatemala in 1523. He divvied up the Indigenous people of the declining Maya culture and their land among his troops. The Spaniards instituted the *encomienda* (a repressive system) in the 16th-17th centuries, which forced the natives to work in the exportation of gold, indigo, and cacao to European markets. There was also history of Guatemalan dictatorships from the 19th-20th centuries: Rafael Carrera, Rufino Barrios, and Manuel Estrada Cabrera. Under the auspices of Cabrera in the early 20th century, the U.S. United Fruit Company obtained large extensions of land for the production of tropical fruits and built a railroad system to facilitate the American business. This represents an example of American imperialism seeking to benefit from an unstable political regime under the rule of Cabrera to enrich the pockets of U.S. businessmen much like the *encomienda* system of the Spaniards.

Sasha noted that recently the current president of Guatemala Jimmy Morales is being investigated by the ICAC, which was instituted in Guatemala in 2007. This commission was successful in ousting the former president Otto Pérez Molina on deceitful unscrupulous charges. Morales is being investigated for receiving illicit campaign funds from a well-known drug trafficker. Morales is fervently trying to demine the value of the international commission by declaring it defunct and cowardly dishonorable. He attempted to manipulate and gain favor from the Trump administration by supporting the controversial relocation of Israel's capital this past year.

Although the U.S. has supported the ICAC in Guatemala and other Central American countries by contributing $2 billion, it has emphasized the debate over the wall on its border with Mexico as the optimum solution. The U.S. should continue its efforts to combat the Satanic sordid venality, the root cause of illegal immigration from Guatemala to the U.S.; it should also acknowledge its role in exploiting Guatemala for profit during the inception of the United Fruit Company that acquired large portions of land for its benefit while contributing to the debt and economic instability of this country.

Unfortunately, it is easy to simplify the border crisis and reduce it to blaming one political party or another on the fear of the "browning" of America. The real "identify crisis" is turning a blind eye to the historical causes of the crumbling putrescence in Guatemala in which the U.S. also played a part. Sasha and Marcos were aware the U.S. was cognizant of the malfeasant shadiness in Guatemala and other countries in Central America, but many journalists and politicians focus more on the wall and racial issues like this one. It is difficult and complex for the U.S. and the international community to fight corruption in the Northern Triangle of Central America (Guatemala, Honduras, and El Salvador), but Marcos agreed with Rafael that this has to be at the forefront of the immigration conversation.

REPARATIONS AND LIBERAL DEMOCRATS

THEY ALSO NOTED that Julián Castro, who is running as a Democratic presidential candidate in 2020, is in favor of paying repatriation costs for the Black slaves. Is he proposing this because he wants to gain their vote, or does he really care for the "slaves"? It would seem appropriate to discuss the economic damage the United Fruit Company created in Central America in the 20th century. Shouldn't the Democrats also discuss how the U.S. enslaved the Indigenous and poor Central Americans as the UFC acquired vast amounts of land and supported the *encomienda* system where the poor were forced to work the plantations and build the railroads? Shouldn't repatriation payments also be offered to the indigent and poor of Central America? Many think the immigration crisis wouldn't be so bad if the U.S. wouldn't have imposed their will on these countries to earn a buck off of their sweat and sacrifice. It is evident the U.S. oversimplifies the immigration crisis by narrowing it down to race and whether a wall should be constructed or not.

Marcos was following the announcement by Robert Francis O'Rourke by which he confirmed he was also running as a Democratic presidential candidate for the 2020 campaign. It was interesting to note the underlying prejudice of Rubén Navarrette, a syndicated columnist for The Washington

Post, that describes O'Rourke, nicknamed Beto, as a liberal of White privilege. He is the son of Pat O'Rourke, a former El Paso County judge and county commissioner. Pat believed the "Beto" moniker, according to Navarrette, would fool Mexicans into believing he was a Latino in order to gain their votes. Navarrette also disclosed that Beto retired from the House of Representatives after three two-year terms where he didn't pass any significant bills, and he avoided the immigration issue and did not reach out to Latinos. Furthermore, Navarrette mentioned that Beto disclosed his personal wealth of between $5 million to $10 million, and he spent three months traveling the country to find America and to possibly find himself. Only someone of White privilege, according to Navarrette, could afford to do this. Navarrette, conversely, believes that Julián Castro is a true Latino. Marcos agreed that Castro is a Latino due to his skin color, but a "true" Latino is questionable because he is not fluent in Spanish. Without this ability to speak Spanish, Castro cannot penetrate the veneer of the unmistakable Hispanic culture, especially, since it means discussing the immigration issue with leaders of Mexico and Central America.

It's funny that Navarrette describes the Cinco de Mayo celebration as a fake Mexican holiday created by White people to celebrate beer in his article, "Beto born to run—as whatever you want." (March, 2019) He further adds that it would be a great day to kick off the candidacy of a bogus candidate (Beto) adored by White Liberals. Everyone knows that Beto is an Irish American. What's interesting is that Beto probably speaks more Spanish than Julián Castro who pretends to be Hispanic. Wouldn't it have been more appropriate for Castro to have announced his candidacy during the St. Patrick's Day celebration since he's not "genuinely" a Hispanic? However, Castro announced his intentions to run for office at the iconic Virgen de Guadalupe Plaza in San Antonio a few months ago. Marcos did not think any Hispanic fell for his hypocrisy and phoniness.

AMERICA'S SPIRITUAL CHALLENGES

MARCOS AND HIS friends loved speculating about the future of America and its relationship with the rest of the world. They realized we still live in a "global community" of us versus them. The recent tragic killing of 50 or more Muslims in New Zealand by a right nationalist, White-lone gunman shook the nation. Many newsmen stated he was inspired by people like President Trump, who has used rhetoric in the past, accusing all Muslims of being terrorists and Mexicans being criminals and rapists. Even though Liberals try to blame Trump for the ills of the world, which is wrong because they are promoting their limited personal agenda. The best approach should be to not fight evil-vile atrociousness but to embrace iniquity with love. This is what Martin Luther King Jr. advocated, but more importantly, this is what Jesus championed. In Matthew 5:45 it states, "He causes his son to rise on the evil and the good." According to Wayne W. Dyer, it's extremely paramount "to practice nonresistance because this tells us to bring the spirit of God to all perceived evil, and that alone will transform it into good." He mentions this maxim in his book *There's a Spiritual Solution to Every Problem*. There is no doubt Trump could use "softer words" when he addresses legal or illegal immigrants flooding through the borders of the U.S. It is a reminder to all of us to choose our "morphemic lexical structures" more sagaciously as we confront one another with our differences in opinion.

All of us must constantly look within to access our spiritual gift, which is given to us naturally. We have to remember that the spirit of God dwells within us instead of outside of us as Dyer and many others, like Mother Teresa, remind us. The battle is won with love, and it's such a difficult concept for all of us to master. Love dissolves all fear, doubt, and disharmony in our lives. As Rafael sat with his friends, Marcos, Sasha, and his wife, he realized that love had to be the final word in the end. Love is a word celebrated each Sunday in all of our churches, synagogues, temples, and other worship centers in America and throughout the world, but its essence is so difficult to practice in our daily lives, which are afflicted with problems we all must address.

Love is the ointment that soothes and heals the wounds of the human soul. Rafael was reminded of the rejuvenating nature of love as he struggled on his Cervélo triathlon bicycle on a 70-mile ride east of Cibolo, riding through the breezy country roads east of IH-10 on the back roads leading to Seguin, Texas. The fields were plentiful with blankets and oceans of wildflowers: bluebonnets, Indian paint brush, and purple and yellow flowers lining the roads. Each year God reminds us of his love as the earth shows its reassuring colors amidst the flooding in Nebraska and the other disasters like the tsunami that devastated islands in Indonesia. We ask the question again and again, "Why the destruction and suffering God?" God reminds us to dwell in tender affection for there will be heartache and destruction in this life. It is a reminder to look within where the spirit resides, and He wants us to rest in his peace when disaster strikes. This ability to rely solely on God through the ups and downs of life is the *bona fide* challenge for all of us.

Josefina believed it required a veritable discipline and practice to access the fountain of "delightful enchantment." A distracted mind can lead us astray. The mind must be trained much like an athlete trains his/her body to perform. There is a time to push and a time to rest. The mind also needs the transcendence of meditation to fuel it with positive thoughts to counterbalance the negativity that invades our spiritual realm of being. Our society beguiles us from the peace we are dependent to rely on. In a city like San Antonio, for instance, like any big city there are places like the ubiquitous gentlemen's clubs that allure lonely men to their doors. Inside the establishment they can drink alcohol and satisfy their carnal desires watching women strip as they dance around silver-plated poles on their tall stiletto heels, exposing their full-body dangling breasts, Botox-filled asses, and shaven vaginas. Long hair sways through the dark light sprinkled with reflections of mirrors and flicking colors of light on long and rounded earrings, enticing the men's eyes and thus increasing the blood flow filling the bulge in their pants. The attraction of tattoos etched into the skin of their bodies adds an exotic dimension to their desire. A yearning reflected in the diamond stud embedded in their belly buttons. A sensual craving alleviated by the hard erection exploding to the tantalizing visuals imposed on the mind. An explosion that soon fades and leaves them wasted and empty. An emptiness that needs to be filled with the same panacea over and over again. Mankind is overtaken with this type of destruction, which can take shape in many different forms, whether it's a result of overworking, overeating, overdrinking, over worrying, or any other vice that consumes us. They keep us from living in the space of peace, comity, love, and tranquility.

Sasha agreed that we all have choices to make as to what we choose to do every given minute of each day. In our society we are flooded with decisions to honor, and social media sometimes exasperates this area of our personal and social lives. Many are attracted to the status it gives us by receiving the most "likes" or approvals from others after posting a beautiful picture from a trip to exotic and wonderful places, whether it be in Portugal, the hills of France, or a fun-filled day at Disney World. We want people to know what we are doing to reinforce our identity and validity to friends and ourselves. The social pressures of revealing ourselves to others is real and dangerous to our souls. This is why it's essential to have this verbal exchange with ourselves and others according to Sasha and her friends.

In the beginning, according to Genesis, the seas, land, animals, and sky were created in a span of a week. The seventh day was established as a day of rest and self-reflection. It was a day of thanksgiving and of honoring the Creator, God. *Dios* then created man, and from his rib he created woman. What a wonderful gift God gave to the world! As a result, the final word is to continue this discourse about the human condition: its challenges, failures, and rewards. The "remonstrance" is also to trust, have faith; ultimately, love no matter what happens in this life. Rafael was reminded of an experience he shared with a mother from Laredo at a mental health facility on Fredericksburg Road in San Antonio this past week. She was there waiting with her son, an adult now, who suffered from a mental health issue. Rafael was there as a Spanish interpreter to help her understand the doctor who only spoke English while she only spoke Spanish.

Rafael and the mother, in her early 70s, had an interesting and compelling chat in Spanish as they waited in a small enclosed waiting area with no windows and full of patients in chairs cluttered together. The mother described the life lesson she learned working as a caregiver. She cared for a 90-year-old woman who was bound to a wheelchair. The lady was able to get herself in and out of bed, but she never complained about her declining health. The mother would ask her if she would prefer to be with her children and grandchildren, and the lady said, "I don't want to sit in front of them all day and have them feel sorry for me. They have busy lives, going to school and working." The elderly lady indicated that she visited with them from time to time, but there was no need to live with them. The mother, who cared for her, helped with light cleaning around the house and cooking. They would watch the elderly lady's favorite *telenovela* every afternoon at 2 p.m. The lady left an indelible impression on the woman Rafael spoke to that afternoon. Her positive attitude and complete trust in God inspired her to live her life fully and without regrets.

Josefina listened to her husband as he recalled his colloquy with the lady at the doctor's office. His story caused her to reminisce about a church outing she had this past weekend with her friend Estela. Since Rafael was out of town participating in a triathlon, she would sometimes get together with Estela. They attended the 5 p.m. church service on Saturday at the large Community Bible Church on 1604 and Redline Rd. The minister preached from the book of Jonah, the prophet who was prompted by God to go to Nineveh. Jonah disobeyed God by boarding a boat that was sailing to Tarshish, a city far away from where God wanted him to go. The Israelites from Nineveh had just been defeated and decimated by another culture, but God wanted Jonah to go there to spread the good news of the

Gospels. ***Jehová*** wanted him to show his love for his enemies, so they could see the power and gracious nature of the Lord. Jonas thought he could hide from God, but as the biblical story unfolds, ***El Señor*** was omnipresent even as Jonas was swallowed by the whale. God was present even in the belly of the big fish, and this is where Jonas knew that he must obey God's command for his life. Many times we act like Jonas when we try to walk away or hide from our problems. Our quandaries will always exist, but *Dieu* wants to walk with us as we learn to love our personal enemies and to help us face our individual obstacles.

After the service, Josefina and Estela went to a restaurant that served a Louisiana cuisine. They enjoyed an appetizer of shrimp nachos with finely sliced tomatoes and lettuce as they drank a smooth but rich glass of cabernet sauvignon. They pondered this concept of the Great Commission in which God commanded his people to create new churches all over the world to spread the Gospel of Jesus Christ. Estela wondered, "How would this affect people from other cultures who practice Islam,

Buddhism, Hinduism, Judaism, and other religions?" As a Christian she was in agreement in spreading the love of Jesus to others, but could it be possible that this could present itself as an encroachment upon other faiths? Josefina opined that the discrepancy would be Christianity would not be forced upon others, but that it would exist for others to experience the love of God. As a result, people would be able to choose for themselves as to what faith to espouse. So many leave their former religious practice to become Christians, and others may refuse Christianity. For others, the Gospel would be introduced to them for the first time; therefore, they could choose whether to believe in Jesus or not. They both agreed Christianity or any other religion should not be forced on others, whether they are nonbelievers or members of another faith. The love of God instructs us to *amar a otros* (to love others) others regardless of their religious beliefs. At least, one could foment and cherish the ubiquitous message of shared brotherhood and peace that is the common denominator among all religions of the world.

THE DANGERS OF FUNDAMENTALISM

RELIGIONS BECOME DANGEROUS when groups of people become fundamentalists, believing their faith is the only way. This perilous approach only creates divisions and hate, as witnessed during the Inquisition period of the Middle Ages. During this time, people of other faiths (primarily Jews and Muslims) were tortured and killed for not professing their allegiance to Christianity or, specifically, to the Catholic Church. In our modern era, we can witness this type of fundamentalism from the Islamic State of Iraq and Syria (ISIS) and other groups like the right-wing Anglo-Saxon group that is anti-Semitic and exclusive of other ethnic groups other than the White-European race. The Ku Klux Klan is another example of a group using Christianity as a shield to promote hatred and racism, primarily, against Blacks, but also against other ethnic groups. This is abhorrent and must be confronted with love at all costs.

The dilemma, of course, as it surfaced in many discussions between Josefina and Rafael, is how does one fight the Islamic State in the Middle East when it kills and attacks people in Iran and Syria for not adhering to their fundamentalist philosophy? How does the world exchange love for a vicious campaign that utilizes hate and destruction to advance their formula of religion and a political state? Should the U.S. military and other democratic nations continue in the long-protracted war against terrorists and ISIS in Afghanistan, Syria, and Iran? These are questions that we must contend with and figure out. Can we truly overcome the threat of ISIS wanting to spread its terror throughout the world with the sword of love? Why do and should countries, like the U.S., spend billions of dollars on the military if we are nations of love? These are the dilemmas that we, as a nation and as Christians, must address.

Should we stand around with signs *a la Woodstock* of harmony, peace, and *amour* with long hair and bare feet *a la Purple Haze* of Jimi Hendrix's, the stamped and sealed metaphor engraved for eternity in the historic pages of music, depicting the infamous turbulence of the late 1960s and 70s as we smoke a doobie and return to being or not being the nostalgic sardonic hippies on an epic groovy period and psychedelic journey in our American history's psyche—Right on Bro—as we disarm our military? Should our government wave a huge sign of "deep affection and loving fondness" in front of Kim Jong-un of North Korea who continues to build his military and advances his nuclear arms development with the sole intent of obliterating into shreds the United States of America? According to Rafael, we should all ponder these questions as Christians and non-Christians. Does an agenda of love include war and defending our rights of freedom and liberty for all? How is this accomplished in a complex and divergent world? Yes, it begins in the individual by nourishing peace and love within, and from here it could be spread from one individual to another. The purpose behind the Great Commission is to spread the Gospel and good news to all men/women of every nation throughout the world. But how does this commission spread and grow in places of the world where there is hostility and violence? It seemed like part of the answer rests in the fact that countries like the U.S. need to maintain a strong military to preserve their freedoms and enter other areas of the global community when solicited by other nations because their rights and individual freedoms are being violated. Is it possible that war could be a demonstration of love?

How would Mahatma Gandhi and Martin Luther King Jr. react to the harmonious brotherhood by combating the enemy of love by means of war and weapons of destruction? Should one pray and meditate as we are lined up and slaughtered by the enemy? Will this change his heart to become more empathetic and accepting of others as he watches us die in a nonresistant manner? These are onerous "platitudes" to embrace as we confront the violence and rigorous hardships of the world. How does a world love ISIS, an organization that beheads people who oppose their ideology? If an Afghan woman were to try to work outside of the house or attend school, would she be killed and stoned by ISIS? Can this type of evil and oppression be combated with weapons of love? Americans can rub shoulders with their hostile and cowardly foes, in this case ISIS, but how do we and other nations help preserve the human rights of all individuals? Is ISIS an organization that wishes to dialogue and share their medieval-antiquated-patriarchal perspective of culture and traditions with others? These are complex inquiries we should all ponder and investigate.

As Sasha carefully deliberated on this serious "motif" with Rafael, she wondered if war, in this case, was necessary to retain the affinity we feel for others, especially our hostile adversaries. If ISIS could allow people to choose their own way of life, maybe there would be more Islamic people joining their community. But it seemed clear to Rafael that ISIS and other extremists should be peaceful in their approach. Now, that ISIS is defeated in Racha, Syria, wouldn't it be a good time to embrace former members of this terrorist group with love and compassion? Nevertheless, if they are still intent on attacking and murderously decapitating "unsullied" Syrian civilians, especially vulnerable and highly intelligent women and innocent children (compared to the bestiality of men in general), ISIS and its radical and nonhuman and merciless tactics as 'satanic mercenaries of unrelenting death' upon the weak and vulnerable must be destroyed. *Hay un tiempo para matar y tiempo para curar; tiempo para destruir, y tiempo de edificar.* (There is "[a] time to kill, and a time to heal; a time to break down, and a time to build up.") Ecclesiastes 3:3 Lives must be protected at all costs, whether ISIS or any other cowardly extremists and despicable terrorists of the worst kind believe this nor not.

CENTRAL AMERICAN GANGS AND AMERICAN IGNORANCE

ANOTHER CRISIS SEEMS to be getting worse by the day along the U.S. and Mexican border. Thousands of Central American illegal immigrants are converging on the perimeter to seek asylum from the Northern Central American Triangle (Honduras, Guatemala, and El Salvador) where gangs control the streets and survive by extortion and violent coercion. Just recently, Marcos viewed a piece on the news covering the MS-13 gangs in Guatemala targeting young adolescent boys to join their *pandillas*. The boy was taken to an abandoned house where he was tortured by cigarette burns to his upper torso, and they were going to chop off his hands with a machete for refusing to join their group. The boy's mother happened to call the police, which no one can trust because of the high level of corruption in these countries, but by the grace of God, the police did follow up on this call. They were able to save the innocent boy from the injuries the gang members were getting ready to inflict on him.

Sasha realized there was no easy fix for the immigration crisis. Not only did it relate to nefarious unprincipled government officials, gangs, and drug cartels, but it was also exasperated by American journalists who falsely believed they understood the contentious matters. She found it interesting to learn of Rubén Navarrette, a nationally recognized columnist who writes on issues pertaining to Latinos. By some he might be considered an expert, but after reading some of his excerpts, it is evident that he is blindsided by his limited experience with policies pertaining to Mexico and Latin America. He was born in Fresno, California and graduated from Harvard. However, he is handicapped by his inability to speak Spanish, and he feels uncomfortable when travelling to Mexico, for example, because he is Mexican American and not Mexican. Octavio Paz, the renown and illustrious Mexican author, describes Hispanics like Navarretti as *Pochos*, Hispanics raised in the U.S. who do not speak a lick of Spanish (*no hablan ni pío de español*); any many times Pochos are extreme racists against national Mexicans or any other Latin American who speaks fluent español o castellano.

En las calles (streets) using the "academic vernacular" of this arena, so to speak, Mr. Navarretti would be depicted as would be Julián and Joaquín Castro, the other "liberal monolingual political clown and twin brothers" from San Antonio, Texas's (*clásico puro shine órale, Ese...*) Westside, as well as Alexandria Ocasio-Cortez, who struts her corpulent booty with no salsa *ritmo*, as cocos (coconuts)—white on the inside and brown on the outside. René Marqués, the well-versed Puerto Rican writer from the early 20th century, redacted *La carreta*, which depicts the surge of immigrants to places like New York. Ocasio-Cortez is a Nuyorican who speaks in proper español and despises national Puerto Rican born and raised Boricuas from the idyllic Pearled Island of the Caribbean, Puerto Rico.

Many in American society, who are ignoramus, mistakenly believe Harvard University and Stanford in California, where the twin-*payasos* with *caras de nopales* (faces of the Mexican cactus Nopal) from San Antonio, the preceding Liberal American Socialists and their alma matters are the high standard of any Ivy League university in the U.S. and the rest of the global community.

Unfortunately, these phony academic institutions are probably the worst in modern or past existence because of their inability to dialogue philosophically with their students incorporating the principles of Socrates, Plato, and Aristotle and many others like Jean Jacques Rousseau, Voltaire, and Francisco Arriví—for instance—who wrote *La máscara puertorriqueña* and underlines in this play the lack and racist avoidance of what he refers to and coins as *Sincretismo cultural* because many Puerto Ricans and

Neyoricans like his heroine Cambucha cover their beautiful *trigueñoa* (light dark) skin with white powder to appear as a Whiter Puerto Rican, male or female. Ocasio-Cortez is Cambucha, basically a racist against Afro-Puerto Ricans and the indigenous Puerto Rican *taínos*, which translates into an extreme racist bigotry towards any minority in the U.S.—African Americans, Latinos, Native Americans, and the many other Asian minorities.

These aforementioned Liberal Socialist Marxist Democratic Cocos and Cambuchas like the American Hispanics (Navarretti, the Castros, and Ocasio-Cortez along with the whole racist and prejudiced Biden and Obamas' Political party), not founded on Jesus Christ and His radical principles of racial and ethnic equality, as proposed by Martin Luther King Jr. rather the extreme opposite as propagated by the incompetent unconscious Joe Biden and his highly intellectual love for pistachio ice cream and his Son Hunter, extremely ugly pretending to be James Dean with a pencil-neck body and a fraudulent drug addict extorting money from Russia, China, Kyrgyzstan, and many other countries in Eastern Europe to fill his pockets to sustain his cocaine addiction. Lack of coolness as a dumb ignoramus monolingual crack head—the ultimate false bogus standard of today's Liberal Democratic Party—a complete joke and ultimate embarrassment that has ever been witnessed in American's political history in 2024, making the Mexican Drug Lord El Chapo seem like a model citizen compared to the Satanic worshipping Democratic Satanic Socialist Party of 2024 under the incompetent Biden's Evil Administration of 2024.

Furthermore, the Obamas live with the rich in Martha's Vineyard and not in Chicago, where they are from not doing a thing (*ni pío*) about the young Black men who shoot each other very day in the gang related violence ignored for years by the Bidens and Obamas (Barrack a pencil-neck swaying forefinger who doesn't speak Spanish or French—basically incompetent who can't even bench press twenty pounds, but pretends to be athletic, please) do absolutely nothing; as far as the border dividing the U.S. from Mexico and the Latin and Central American is concerned, they have done more harm than good by supporting the corrupt governments of those countries, especially aiding López Obrador and the new presidenta Claudia Sheinbaum—corrupt members of the PRI (*Partido Revolucionario Institucional*) that have coordinated with drug cartels since the end of the

Mexican Revolution of 1921 to traffic young children to the pedophiles in the United States and the rest of the global community, as represented in the movie *Sound of Freedom*. This monolingual racist Liberal Democratic machine is satanic under the leadership of Biden, who began his career supporting the KKK and "propping up" African Americans like Kamala Harris who doesn't *hablar ni pío de español* but was going to solve the root "muddle" and complications of the Northern Triangle of Central America (Honduras, Guatemala, and El Salvador) with her screeching hyena laugh, a cartoonist embarrassment of what was once the great United States of America.

The American Socialist-Satanic Liberal Democratic Party, backwards adhering to its basic philosophical suicide, supports a new American socialist and Marxist thinking of the worse kind, worse than Karl Marx and his proposal for Communism after the Second World War beginning in 1945. Now this abhorrent American despicable Democratic party under the Biden racist-monolingual-backwardness founded on lies and deceits can continue working with Presidenta Steunbaum in propagating the racist and sad truth of the trafficking of children as she and her political cabinet receive kickbacks from the Mexican Cartels.

The best Mexican president Benito Juárez is rolling unrestful and uncontrollably in his grave because he was the only Indigenous lawyer-president in this beautiful and resourceful country, a Mestizo from Zacatecas, Mexico who actually fought fiercely for land reforms for the poor Mestizo indigenous people to own their own parcels of land along with the afro-Mexicans and for their equal civil rights by rewriting the Mexican Constitution of the 1860s since these non-White Mexicans were oppressed during the whole historical account of Mexico, beginning in the 16th century with the arrival of Hernán Cortés to Veracruz and continuing in the later 19th century all the way to the present with the PRI, the Catholic Church, the whiter fraudulently unprincipled-satanic Mexican elite, and the Cartels.

Harvard is a breeding academic pool of racism of the worst kind. They don't believe in free thought as countered, for instance, by Harry Truman who educated himself as a bibliophile from Independence, Missouri; he is considered one of the best U.S. presidents the North America has ever voted democratically into office. Conversely, today, President Biden is the worse president of this once great country as he and his ignoramus cohorts have splintered and divided distastefully all of the states and people of America. Truman unlike Biden, who has created the war in Israel today, had to act decisively without wavering by ordering the unprecedented dropping and release of the atomic bombs on Nagasaki and Hiroshima, Japan with its disastrous outcome, ending horrifically the Second World War beginning in 1945. Moreover, Biden and his "monolingual troops" have created World War III.

Luis Muñoz Rivera is considered the George Washington of Puerto Rico, who was a poet, bibliophile, and the primary author of the *Estado Libre Asociado* (Commonwealth) for this Caribbean island in 1952; thus, he ended the American or *Gringo and Yankee Imperialist rule* by the U.S., a monolingual country with great potential but stagnated in a quagmire of "intellectual suicide" by not being able and with no desire to dialogue with Puerto Rico in Spanish, which would really prove to the island that American diplomats and politicians really respect the *Boricua* islanders by speaking their Spanish language *y en aprender su historia en el idioma castellano* (by learning their history and Castilian or Spanish language) also.

The ignorant decision by American citizens—as a whole, but primarily made by politicians who do not care to learn fluently a foreign language, like Spanish and French, for example, leaves these government officials of the present Democratic Party, as witnessed clearly today in 2024, as being extremely incompetent and destructively and irresponsibly unqualified to lead, what was once the great United States of America. Furthermore, the Democrats do not demonstrate any desire to discuss philosophical, political, or cultural "affairs" in a foreign language ever, and this places all Americans and the rest of the world of "metamorphosing" into a poor and divided Third World country.

Mr. Navarrette is a prime example of this cocky and aggrandized monolingual-racist-*pocho* lens by which he ignorantly patronizes the global community and America with his "Ivy League English only handicap" and extremely stupid ignorance as a *Coco Rico Pero Agrio* (deliciously rich but bitter coconut—*blanco en el interior pero café o pardo en el exterior* (White in the interior and Brown on the exterior). Mr. Pocho-Coquito Navarretti has it wrong in promoting this type of bigotry and racism against all national Latinos and Hispanics, as he claims to be an expert, which he is not, of the Mexican-American and Mexican conundrum, one he will never comprehend unless he gets off his **Coconut High Caballo** and does at least a ten year hiatus in Mexico, Puerto Rico, or any Spanish only speaking country in the world to become fluent in the language and to desire then to *parler* (Converse) with Hispanics fluent in their Spanish language who can express political-cultural-philosophical viewpoints the monolingual academic Navarretti could never penetrative nor understand to work towards peace, harmony, and a justice system that does not condone the corruption and the extreme sexual abuse of children by pedophiles in the United States and globally.

He criticizes and satirizes presidential candidates like Robert Francis O'Rourke who is Irish American but goes by "Beto." He states that O'Rourke pretends to be Latino, but my question is who is Mr. Navarrette bluffing and posing to be? Navarrette seems to disvalue his Hispanic heritage in which his grandfather emigrated from Chihuahua, Mexico to the U.S. He pokes fun of Mexicans, when accused of being Mexican, as wearing a *serape* with a large sombrero with his burro, Pepe, sitting nearby as he pecks away on his laptop. It bothers Navarrette that Beto speaks fluent Spanish; thus, it is his assumption Beto impersonates a Latino. Nevertheless, Navarrette supports Julián Castro as a viable Latino candidate because of his ethnic heritage, being Mexican American, yet neither Castro nor Navarrette speaks Spanish.

I would think Navarrette would embrace Beto for speaking Spanish fluently, regardless of his Irish American ethnicity. This allows him to communicate directly to Hispanics in the U.S. who are fluent in both English and Spanish. It establishes a bond and respect for those wanting to preserve their Latino identity as they assimilate to the American way of life. Octavio Paz, the Mexican author and philosopher, describes the chasm between the Chicano and Mexican American who have become Americanized by only learning English and by inserting a few words here and there in Spanish like, "I'm taking my burro to *la tienda.*" As a "voice" for the *mexicano*, Paz and Mexicans feel disrespected.

This is an important issue especially if one is running for public office or opining as a nationally acclaimed journalist, specializing on Latino issues. Mexican Americans, who adamantly oppose learning Spanish, establish a rift between themselves and Mexican and other Latino nationals. Navarrette exploits the implied racism and ethnic divisions between Whites, Latinos, and African Americans, a learned skill purported in Ivy League institutions, while dismissing the bigoted dissension between Mexican Americans and Mexicans.

As Ortega y Gasset, the Spanish philosopher, might have said, "It's easier to look at others' deficiencies than to *ensimismarse* (to look within)." We should all take a moment to *ensimismarnos* (to look within ourselves) to better "fathom with greater insight" and to relate to others more effectively and empathetically.

Rafael observed that many people, who have graduated from Ivy League universities like Harvard, are molded exclusively in terms of becoming Liberals and Conservatives, Hispanics and Whites, and Whites and African Americans. Felicity Huffman and Lori Loughlin, two Hollywood actresses, paid William "Rick" Singer, who ran a small college preparation company in Newport Beach, California, between $100,000 to $25 million to have their children admitted to Ivy League universities, such as Yale and Stanford. This business provided bribes, phony test takers, and even doctored photos of nonathletic students as athletes to receive scholarships. This was the largest college entrance scam unveiled in U.S. history in March 2019. In Rafael's mind, this type of structured thinking and hoaxing to graduate from coveted Ivy League academic institutions in the U.S. stagnate the intellectual capabilities of the American elite, those who have graduated from Harvard, Yale, Stanford, and other *pretenciosas universidades* (pretentious universities). There are obvious exceptions to this rule, but by and large, elites socialize and study with the same "monochromatic culture;" thus, they adhere to what is obvious to most, many "bogus high-grade and haughty" graduates. They have not become captains of their own ship as Henry David Thoreau would ask each one of us to be. However, they follow the orders of one *capitán* and thus replicate the propagandized viewpoints that have been passed down to them by their professors and business associates. Some like Julián Castro, a graduate of Harvard, will support reparations paid to the ancestors of Black slaves, but why not consider paying reparations to the Native American tribes and the thousands of immigrants fleeing countries in South America, Central America, and Mexico to come to the U.S.? Why not discuss the fraudulent misappropriation and squandering of the United

Fruit Company that capitalized and abused the workers of countries like Guatemala, El Salvador, Honduras, Costa Rica, and countries from the Caribbean, such as the Dominican Republic and Puerto Rico? It was a merchant of evil affiliating itself with the highfalutin aggrandized landowners and cowardly dictators of these countries in the 20th century to build railroads to transport and export bananas and sugarcane all around the world while they made a profit and left the working class stricken with poverty and no labor unions to strike. This type of fraudulent misappropriation and squandering is one of the reasons these countries are unstable and now controlled by "lowlife illiterate, effeminate, and brain deficient" gangs and drug cartels who soil their Mickey Mouse underwear on a good day.

Why isn't Castro discussing this historic event of economic imperialism by the U.S in these countries? Rafael believed it is due to Castro's inability and unwillingness to learn Spanish and connect more profoundly with these Latinos. It's a prejudiced view shared by many Mexican Americans, who prefer to be like White Americans, but some want to be regarded as Hispanics because of the color of their skin and origins as Spanish speakers first and English second. They pretend to be someone they are not.

The Chicano movement in the 1960s was imperative in establishing the rights of Mexican Americans in American society. Leaders like César Chávez in Delano, California and Rodolfo "Corky" Gonzales in Colorado led the way. Corky gained national attention for the poem he wrote, "I am Joaquín" in which he crystallized the sensitivity of the Chicano movement of the time. He identified as a son of the Aztecs and of a North American society that doesn't accept him even after serving his country with sweat and blood during the Vietnam War. He also fought for improved educational, employment, and housing opportunities for Chicanos in Denver. In 1964 President Lyndon B. Johnson passed legislation for the War on Poverty, and Corky was appointed director of Denver's War on Poverty. He soon became disillusioned with politics and founded the Crusade for Justice in 1966. Its goal was the creation of self-determination and community control in all areas of Chicano life. It established its own school, art gallery, *El Gallo* (a newspaper), and credit bureau. In 1968 Gonzales and some of his associates participated in a riot that broke out at West High School in Denver when students walked out to protest the inferior education they were receiving at the school. In 1972 Corky created the Colorado chapter for all Latinos, La Raza Unida Political Party.

Sasha was perplexed by the dichotomies of American society. Many of her Mexican-American friends have either forgotten, ignored, or are unaware of the plight of the Chicano movement. They identify as Navarrette and Castro do as Mexican Americans who are more American than Mexican. Their inability to speak Spanish and their disassociation with Latinos from Spanish speaking countries from Mexico, Central and Latin America, and Spain are evident. Ted Cruz, the newly elected Texas senator, is another example of a Cuban whose father emigrated from Cuba. Cruz speaks very little Spanish; as a result, he is ineffective when addressing issues pertaining to Hispanics, such as immigration policies in the U.S. Speaking Spanish isn't the only qualifier for a Hispanic politician, but Sasha opined that it lets one know where one's heart is.

RIDING, TRIATHLONS, AND FLOW OF CONSCIOUSNESS

AMERICANS ENJOYED MANY freedoms, but Sasha and her friends thought it was essential to have these discussions to preserve our heritage founded on liberty, equality, and justice for all. Rafael pondered these ideals yesterday as he ventured out on a 60-mile bike ride on his *Cervélo* P-5 racing bicycle on the country roads east of IH-10 leading to Zuehl, New Berlin, and the outskirts of Seguin, Texas. The asphalt roads were a little rough and uneven in areas, which made for an arduous but safe ride due to reduced vehicular traffic. The strong head and crosswinds were the real challenge because the rider had to focus on maintaining his balance and sustained effort. Many of the fields near New Berlin were blanketed with Indian paintbrush flowers with patches of thick bluebonnets. There was also an array of buttercup flowers in white, purple, and rose colors decorating the Texas landscape. He encountered a big turtle crossing the road, and he always stopped to transport the meditative animal hiding within its shell to the safety of the tall grass on the other side of the sizzling speckled gray-black-white asphalt pavement. His shell was wet and shiny after surviving the deluge of the previous day. The scenic terrain was also peppered with views of wooden fences, horses, and cows feeding in the pastures. At 61 years of age, Rafael enjoyed the freedom of being able to go for a bike ride in the middle of the day. He worked sporadically as an interpreter for schools and medical clinics, but it was not a hectic pace as when he worked full-time as a schoolteacher in English, Spanish, and French and as an Adjunct Spanish Professor at the university level teaching Spanish grammar and Hispanic literature.

However, the routine could get a little monotonous like anything else in life. Other responsibilities like projects around the house, cooking more for Josefina, who stilled worked full-time as a medical doctor, and caring for his elderly parents and sister, who suffered from a mental illness and with renal failure on dialysis, could be taxing at times. It also would sometimes affect his marriage just because there were always issues to address, like taking his sister, Rebecca, to the pool and gym often to exercise. The need to entertain his parents as well as Rebecca with activities like going to church, the movies, concerts, and other events, such as a San Antonio Spurs and high school basketball games, primarily with his father only. Rafael and Josefina also took his family to plays and ballet performances, which were also significant and meaningful. It felt good to give and help others, but it was also challenging to balance it all.

Yesterday Rafael participated in the Texas State Triathlon in San Marcos, an event he probably had done now for about 18 years. The cold breeze at 47 degrees spawned his exposed and vulnerable skin to shiver uncontrollably and spasmodically with the thought of jumping into the spring-fed river, which remained at a constant 73 degrees, was daunting especially right at sunrise. Many of the same athletes, such as Raye, Shanan, Guille, Dane, and other triathlete acquaintances with familiar faces and others would show up annually. This was one of the first triathlons of the season in Central Texas. It consisted of a 500-meter swim, 14-mile bike ride, and a 5K run. Rafael was participating in the Aqua bike event, which consisted only of the swim and bike ride. He had not run now for about 8½ months due to a frayed-right foot Achilles tendon triggering a severe, painful, and long-lasting and agonizing tendinitis. It surprised him that it was taking so long to normalize. He missed running, but he was committed to wait until it mended. Rafael had been icing his foot every night, and he also used some electromagnetic treatment from time to time. At the gym he would do his calf raises and stretches, which were supposed to help it heal. Some days it felt pretty good, but on many days, it felt swollen and achy. It seemed like it was not convalescing at all. The Achilles would really sting in the shower when hot water from the showerhead would saturate it. Rafael wasn't angry, but he was mystified by the slow progress of its ultimate improvement.

He often pondered with Josefina about how hard it must be for athletes, professional and recreational, to retire from sport. Not only is the sport a job or hobby, but one also identifies with it. It also becomes a way of living a healthy lifestyle. Returning to San Marcos yesterday to race, Rafael recalled riding his red Motobecane 10-speed down Post Road on his way to Five Mile Dam back in the fall of 1977, 43 years ago. The patchy road had not changed much over the years. The same rusted railroad tracks hung over the byway right before the river crossing. Memories of sitting on the stoned-five-foot dam wall allowing the cool water to soak his legs were refreshing. The recollection of small perch nibbling nervously on his legs was another fond thought. It was interesting to note how the past replays itself in the present, flicking from one slide to another in one's mind and spirit.

As Rafael returned to the present in his flow of consciousness style of ruminating, he reflected on another article by the supposedly "nationally acclaimed" journalist, Rubén Navarrette. In his article, "Given family journey, Romney wrong on refugees." According to Navarrette, Romney, the Utah senator, who ran for candidacy during the 2012 presidential campaign, endorsed the idea of letting the undocumented stay in the U.S. if the southern parameter was secured. Now, Romney supports the Trump campaign of shutting down the border and preventing illegal immigrants from entering the U.S. territory. What's fascinating, according to Rafael, is that Navarrette seems to take a stance against any politician, whether it be Donald Trump, Mitt Romney, or Beto O'Rourke, who happens to be White. Instead of bridging the gap and differences between ethnicities, Navarrette is intent on dividing politicians and focusing on the same old rift as soleless worn out tennis shoes between Democrats and Republicans. His articles lack any sort of critical thinking, which is surprising since he is a graduate of Harvard University.

What is Navarrette's solution to the immigration crisis at the border? He has no solution other than to criticize any stance taken, whether it is to build the wall or not. Navarrette can't relate to the people of Mexico or Central America because he doesn't speak Spanish. His only connection is his grandfather who came from Chihuahua, Mexico to the U.S. as a farmworker during the Mexican Revolution of 1910-1921. Romney's father (former Michigan governor and 1968 presidential candidate) was also born in Chihuahua, Mexico. The funny thing is that Romney probably speaks Spanish whereas Navarrette doesn't. Rafael believed this to be the underlying prejudice as to why Navarrette criticizes White politicians.

If Navarrette spoke Spanish, he could interview Andrés Manuel López Obrador, the current president of Mexico, to get his take on immigration. He could also dialogue with former presidents from Mexico like Peña Nieto and Carlos Salinas, for example, in their native *español*—what a sagacious concept—to better understand the cowardly and unscrupulous deceit of this country south of our border. In his article "Given family journey, Romney wrong on refugees," Navarrette criticizes Mitt Romney for taking a soft stance on immigration. Romney proposed that illegal immigrants should "self-deport."

He also suggested letting the undocumented stay in the United States if the border was secure during the 2012 presidential campaign. Presently, Navarrette accuses Romney of supporting politicians backing President Trump's crusade to shut out immigrants and refugees from countries he deems inferior. Because of his inability to speak Spanish, he can only lambaste other American politicians for their inequities out of his frustration for not understanding Latinos. Navarrette acquired his snobbishness and "higher-than-thou attitude," after graduating from Harvard, a Leftist Socialist Machine; he fervently endeavors to manipulate the American public's opinion in a very blatant, smug, and vain attempt to coerce them to return sublimely to the past era, for example, of a new Biden type-Hitler-Mussolini-Kamala Harris government. Navarrette ineffectively promotes his and the Democratic Left's one-sided approach to control and twist American viewpoints through news agencies and social media outlets like CNN, Facebook, and Navarrette's news-*pocho*-opinion column to develop and indoctrinate Americans to jump on the Socialist agenda bandwagon aligned with those of past fascists and oppressing dictators like Hitler, Mussolini, and Franco in Europe during World War II.

Navarrette detests the Pragmatism of William James—the founding philosophical father of American thought and practice—as he enthusiastically supports the Gringo Leftist-fake-elitists, who rub shoulders with past and present dictators like Fidel Castro and Francisco Maduro, for example, who favor human rights abuses along with the despicable business of trafficking of innocent children for sexual purposes to pedophiles and other disgusting perverts in the United States and abroad. Biden's open border policy, which is a disaster unknown previously in American history, vehemently indulges and worships *la ideología* of Karl Marx. Navarrette intellectually is basically *un bébé qui suce son pouce en couche-culotte* (a baby still sucking his thumb) refusing to learn from Jean Jacques Rousseaux, one of the founding French fathers of democracy as explicated in his book *Social Contract.*

In past articles Navarrette likes to point fingers and condemn politicians like Beto O'Rourke, Donald Trump, and now Romney with whom he disagrees. However, he never presents his point of view in regard to the border crisis. Navarrette also enjoys dwelling on the fear of some Americans of the browning of America; therefore, for some the border must be secured. As a Mexican American, who claims to be more American than Mexican, he narrow-mindedly focuses on racial issues, pitting Whites against Hispanics.

What is Navarrette's solution to the border crisis? He never offers one. Let me assume that he suggests opening the border to all illegal immigrants from Mexico and Central America. After all, Texas, New Mexico, Utah, Colorado, Arizona, Nevada, Wyoming, and California belonged to Mexico before the Treaty of Guadalupe Hidalgo was signed in 1848 after the Mexican-American War of 1846. At this time, the U.S. purchased these vast territories for $15 million. Does Navarrette really care about the plight of Hispanics? He doesn't speak Spanish even though his grandfather was born in Chihuahua, Mexico and came to the U.S at the beginning of the 20th century to work as a farmworker. Navarrette prefers hotdogs to enchiladas and forget the *mole* as he has referenced in previous articles. He doesn't address the political-decaying-putrescence of Central American countries and Mexico, which plays a huge role in the immigration crisis.

Did Navarrette read Octavio Paz's *Laberinto de soledad* or José Vasconcelos's *La raza cósmica*? Or for that matter, has he read "Yo soy Joaquín" by Rodolfo Corky Gonzales during his tenure at Harvard University? He might understand his internal crisis as a Mexican

American, who is more American than Mexican, by reading Paz's book. He would realize he is a *mestizo* (mixed race), an ethnic group that should be embraced, according to Vasconcelos. Finally, he could appreciate the Chicano and Mexican-American struggle from the 60s to the present in which many Hispanics choose to value both cultures with a desire to speak Spanish and English fluently, as suggested by Corky Gonzales. By speaking Spanish, Navarrette could gain a journalistic perspective that is foreign to him.

Yes, Romney's Mormon great-grandfather fled the U.S. in 1885, escaping intolerance and discrimination in the Midwest for a safe haven in Chihuahua, Mexico, the country Trump and Mitt Romney now target to shut down with a wall due to the influx of illegal immigrants.

However, Navarrette tends to find flaws in others at the expense of ignoring his own personal identity crisis as a Mexican American who chooses to build his own internal incarcerated wall instead of a bridge to embrace his dual heritage. He is only fooling himself by sitting on the fence without getting his feet wet on either side of the border barrier. This crisis is a muddy affair skewed by limited perspectives.

The problem with Ivy League schools, according to Rafael, is that they for the most part provide a distorted academic foundation. Journalists like Rubén Navarrette and presidential candidates like Julián Castro, both of whom graduated from Harvard, are Hispanics who have distanced themselves from their roots. They have the *mestizo* skin tone and can speak a few words of Spanish, but they are not fluent. The Ivy League universities focus on the injustices of White society against primarily the Blacks. They mainly focus their attention on political issues to the Left. By reliving the injustices of slavery, for example, they dwell on the past with a burning desire to keep the hatred and wounds alive in the present.

During the 1950s and 60s, it was common for Liberal academic professors to criticize the United States for its imperialistic footprints, "avaricious enterprises", and interferences in Latin America and Third World countries. The fear of communism spreading to countries like Cuba, Nicaragua, and Chile was a target for political Liberals from the Left to criticize the North American monopolistic and tyrannical aggression and involvement in these areas. The failed Bay of Pigs (*Bahía de Cochinos*) invasion of Cuba by the U.S. Army 1961, under the presidency of Dwight

D. Eisenhower, is an example of an imperialistic and forceful intent. One could argue the U.S. government supported Fulgencio Batista, the former Cuban dictator, overthrown by Fidel Castro in 1959. Batista and his supporters benefitted from the U.S. interests on the island related to sugarcane production, hotel investments, and other "educational-retailing-merchant deals" while poverty increased among the working class. The Liberals in a way supported communism to assist the lower class.

When Sasha had these discussions with Rafael, she pointed out that neither the Left nor the Right; neither the Democrats nor Republicans are correct in their assessment of the issues facing our nation and world today. People like Castro and Navarrette are Hispanic by ancestry, for example, but they have colored their skin and identity with the academic values of the White elite. They feel like they are attacking the White establishment and their dominance in politics, but they exacerbate the issues for minorities, especially Hispanics. Castro espouses the teaching of the Catholic Church; however, he is not a practicing Catholic. This would be another common view of Liberals from the Left, who support the separation of state and religion, whereas Conservatives on the Right would favor keeping God and prayer in the public schools across America. Castro is basically saying, "I'm Hispanic but don't speak Spanish; I am Catholic, but I don't practice my faith. However, I do believe in taking care of the poor and treating everyone equally, regardless of racial, social, or economic disparities."

In translation according to Rafael, Sr. Castro is vociferating, "I am a 'poser' (fake) and a *pocho* (a coconut, brown on the outside and white on the inside); yes, I want to line my pockets with a lot of *dinero* and *influencia política* (political influence) to gain your Latino vote to further my Democratic-Socialistic-Fascist-Communist Party and Regime's blueprint for you in America. By doing this, my Liberal Democratic Party (LDP), under the nonexistent pretense of really wanting to assist Hispanics with their 'advancement' in the United States; specifically, in Texas, will only provide the poor with some 'carrots' for economic security and to foster in them the hope of racial equity and more monetary opportunities for all minorities, but especially, for Hispanics and Afro-Americans. This way, they may not prosper but will blindly follow the LDP and the controlling Catholic Church (CC) in favor of keeping you (the poor minority) as indigents, ignorant, and parasites aligned to the Catholic Church. (*No intenten leer sus biblias individualmente; así te siguen oprimiendo la Iglesia Católica y el LDP para que permanezcan en un estado de indigencia total, ignorantes analfabetos y parasitos simbióticos de la Iglesia Católica*—Do not attempt to read your Bibles individually because by not doing so, the CC and LDP can pretend to care for you as they continue to oppress you into becoming completely indigent, ignorant, and parasites of the Catholic Church."

¡Qué Dios los bendiga! (May God Bless all of you!) It was the only Spanish utterance Sr. Julián Castro, with a very poor accent, uttered as he read from an index card when speaking publicly to a full auditorium of Americans like he did in the 2020 Democratic Convention. Rafael and Sasha agreed, "*¡Qué vergüenza es el señor Julián Castro que finge preocuparse del 'bienestar' de los latinos, los hablantes del español o del castellano al igual que de aquellos hispanos que no hablen este idioma derivado del latín, en los Estados Unidos de América*!" (Accordingly, Rafael and Sasha believed Sr. Julián Castro is a complete embarrassment as he pretends to care for the "wellbeing" of Latinos, native speakers of Spanish or Castilian as well as those who do not speak this language derived from Latin, in the United States of America.)

A THIRD POLITICAL PARTY AND THE ABILITY TO SPEAK SPANISH

JOSEFINA AND RAFAEL believed there was a need in America for a third political party to replace both the Democratic and Republic machines. The Right has its faults, especially when we examine the current political climate under President Donald Trump. Trump's desire to spend billions to build a wall along the U.S. and Mexico border while cutting aid to Mexico and the countries of the Northern Central Triangle is a mistake. To label citizens from these countries as all being criminals and inferior is a grave mistake. His knowledge of the history of Latin America is limited and evidently nonexistent. He doesn't speak Spanish and sees no value in doing so. Nevertheless, his inexperience and lack of entente cordiale are no different than that of the Democratic Party. There needs to be a third party that values languages and culture, especially Spanish, since the fastest growing minority group in the U.S. is Hispanic. Other languages are important as well, but it seems like Spanish would be the one of highest priority to learn in the U.S.

Rafael believed Navarrette and Castro didn't learn Spanish because this language was spoken by poor immigrants who are labelled as inferior for speaking their native tongue. Navarrette and Castro wanted to learn English perfectly to fit in with the elite of the U.S. Learning English is a necessity and should be encouraged in America, but learning Spanish has to be an equal priority. To communicate effectively with Obrador, the current president of Mexico, it is essential to speak Spanish even if he speaks English. This establishes a tone of deference and humility by showing that you value him as a person, and you also value his culture. American politics 101 should require a person to speak Spanish. It is demeaning if presidential candidates can only reiterate, *"Sí, se puede"* as Barrack Obama did on occasions or as Castro stated in his Democratic conventions speech of 2016 in which he stated, *"¡Qué Dios los bendiga"*! If you're from the barrio of West Side, San Antonio and your mother was a Chicana activist, it's imperative for you, Castro, to speak Spanish even if it's Tex-Mex.

One could possibly state, *"Dale [shine] a la Virgen de Guadalupe en mi pueblo natal de San Antonio."* That would establish a foundation of respect and honor for the Hispanics of the barrio and the poor who feel disenfranchised from society. Not everyone can attend Stanford and Harvard, but someone like Castro could immerse himself in the barrios across America and the world and reach those in need by speaking to them in Spanish.

Not speaking Spanish or Tex-Mex is like going to war without your sword or weapon. It's like the chisel Michael Angelo needed to carve and create beautiful sculptures of David and others. It's like a fruit tree that doesn't bear fresh fruit. It's like the poet attempting to write poetry with an inkless pen. This is the failure of many Ivy League and other universities that graduate lawyers, who go into politics and separate themselves from the common man, with a camouflaged dream for America. The Castros and Trumps of the world want to appeal to the common man when they are running for elections, but they isolate themselves and their political platforms from their constituents and others when they are elected. This is the problem, and this is why this dialogue, according to Rafael, has no end. It's the continual conversation that's important, and it's one that should not be blindsided by higher institutions indoctrinating their graduates to adapt the left-wing liberal agenda as their political compass.

JARS OF CLAY

THE THICK VEGETATION of early spring enveloped the windows of Josefina and Rafael's dining sunroom. The stained glassed windows on the diced panes facing the backyard displayed the electrifying elegance of loquats hanging with their vibrant yellow colors, sustaining the perspective of the spectator. The highway of branches and leaves decorate the writer's viewpoint wanting to immerse himself in the flood of metaphors. Hints of blue from the sky above peek through the fenestrae rotundas created by homes, arboreal boughs, and the green canopy in the background. During this quiet time before the beginning of the day's activities, Rafael reflects on the verse from 2 Corinthians 4:7, which states, "But we have this treasure in jars of clay' to show that this all-surpassing power is from God and not from us."

Jars are created carefully with fire and the circular molding of clay. Within the jars we hold precious jewels, documents, flowers, or other things we cherish. Ethereally, the spirit of God dwells within the jars like his Essence that lives inside of each one of us. We, as humans, are fragile like the jars, which fall from tables and crack into tiny pieces. However, the Spirit comforts and reminds us of the limitations of this world as God reassures us of the eternal life we will share with him. Jesus shed his blood much like the jars that fall and crack into pieces, but he resurrected on the third day. This reminds us of our rebirth with the Lord once this life on earth vanishes like cracked "jars of clay." Rafael and Josefina were thankful for the hope and faith the Lord's resurgence signifies for all of us. It is the invisible and beautiful treasure within, which we cannot perceive with our senses but know it's there. It's the colorful array of wilting flowers with its cream, purple, red, and violet tones reassuring us of his rebirth. The petals dissipate within the earth, and seeds flourish again into vibrant buds stretching their arms and hands out into existence by painting a dazzling canvas for us all to admire.

Josefina reflected on the execution of the infamous hate crime committed by the racist, John William King, who was administered a lethal dose of pentobarbital yesterday at 6:56 pm; he was pronounced dead twelve minutes later at the Huntsville Unit Prison in Texas on April 24, 2019. He and two others chained James Byrd, an African-American man, to a pickup and dragged him horrifically for three miles until his death on June 7, 1998. It was a modern-day cowardly and heinously-satanic lynching, one that rattled the nation. He was strapped to a gurney with restraints near his wrists and around his waist when the witnesses were ushered into the execution room. Byrd's two sisters and his niece were among the observers as the lethal dose was administered first to his heavily tattooed right arm and then to his left. King showed no remorse as Tiffany Taylor, one of Byrd's sisters, shook her head slowly from side to side. Byrd was dragged until he was dead after being decapitated.

Rafael deduced introspectively the killer "poltroon," whose name is not deserving to be mentioned or known in his life or demise, was crapping in his pants during his moment of death and judgement. Rafael presumed "this lowlife thing" without a sense of right or wrong or a moral compass would be sliced, pulled, and ripped into shreds with a larger-than-life butcher knife and with a grinder eternally slicing this devil-possessed creature with excruciating pain and crunching of the teeth, with a decapitated head and penis, and crying out like a baby while James Byrd rested peacefully in the celestial kingdom of heaven after forgiving him in the only of Jesus Christ. However, neither Josefina nor Rafael knew the heartless killer's heart and whether he had shown remorse bathed in uncontrollable tears for the **pusillanimous** act of murdering an innocent and pure child of God; if he had repented or not. Only God knows the outcome of his ultimate disregard for life by this evil "thing" worse than a pile of excrement flowing from his *boca* (mouth) with serpents eating and feasting grotesquely on his *yeux* (eyes) in Hell.

What an awful act of violence and hatred! One that is seared into the conscious of Byrd's family and the rest of the nation forever. How do we cope, extrapolate, and speculatively conclude and ponder the end result of such a heinous crime? What was the killers' motive? These are just a few of the unanswered questions we all must live with. We reflect on our faith, and we meditate on the image of a *jar of clay*. Mr. King, like all of us, was a child of God. What went wrong? These acts of unconscionable animalistic brutality like the one just reported in the terrorist attack in Sir Lanka on Easter Sunday have been woven into the fabric of our world's tapestry. Innocent people attending a religious ceremony honoring the resurrection of Christ are innocently murdered, a total of approximately 359. Why we ask? These are the interrogative conundrums that keep us awake at night with the recurring nightmares of racism, hatred, and violence. It was evident to Josefina that we need God more than ever in our lives. We cannot afford to distance ourselves from his love and nonviolent and peaceful ways.

Rafael contemplated these issues with Josefina as they drank a warm cup of coffee during the early morning, sharing a moment together in their sunroom. It must pertain to the isolation we feel as humans. We do our own thing and maybe blame others for our failures. We oftentimes live and reside within the boundaries of our prejudiced views, whether they were shaped in academic, ecclesiastical, or secular environments. Many of us don't expose ourselves to travelling to other cultures where diverse languages and traditions are the norm. We are limited by our economic divergences, whether restrained by poverty or wealth. Poverty can contain us in the quagmire of limited social and professional opportunities. Wealth can suffocate us in a bubble of privilege and entitlement like the present scandals among some affluent movie stars paying large sums of money to have their children accepted and enrolled in Ivy League universities. Writers, religious leaders of all faiths, politicians, artists, philosophers, and basically, all people, have the responsibility to discuss and address these issues on a regular basis. These discourses must remain at the forefront of our lives to understand, educate, and promote peace within ourselves and among all people of the world.

As the "jars of clay" are broken and recreated, we must preserve the treasure within, which is God's Spirit. *Le mot de la final* (final "expression") as it is written in the Bible, for instance, is the word that must be read repeatedly. It must be applied in a real and meaningful way to our lives. Church leaders can no longer afford to deliver stale and unstimulating sermons that don't allow us to grow. We need to drink from the "jars of clay" to receive nourishment, knowledge, and growth. Writers need to intentionally "canvass" these matters in their novels, and poets must pursue in their quest of images to diagnose and elevate the metaphors of the human spirit that suffers, cries, mends, rejoices, and resurrects. We must not succumb to laziness as we go to work and perform our daily tasks of living. These activities consume our time, and they are imperative for us to realize and achieve as responsible citizens and family members. However, we must remain vigilant and interact with one another in meaningful ways. Josefina realized that we must bust through the taboo of not "agitating intellectually" the political and racial issues. It's crucial to separate strong feelings from intellectual deliberations. When we discuss and share disparate points of view, without labeling them as right or wrong, we learn from one another in a peaceful and loving manner. Just imagine our nation and world filled with "jars of clay" in an array of disparate colors and shapes, existing harmoniously side by side in our wholeness and raggedness with God's guiding hands molding and reshaping us.

CONVERSATIONS

SASHA AND EFRAÍN, another good friend of Josefina and Rafael, agreed wholeheartedly with Josefina's philosophy and belief. They would all gather once a month at the local coffee house on Broadway St. next to Bike World in the Alamo Heights neighborhood of San Antonio. They would usually meet early on a Saturday morning before Josefina would head off to play tennis at the Sonterra Country Club; before Rafael would go on a 50 to 60-mile bike ride in Cibolo, Texas. In a few weeks, Josefina and Rafael would be travelling to Croatia via Rome for a two-week vacation. They would spend one week on a biking tour with Backroads cruising by bike along the Dalmatian Coast. They will be outfitted with road bikes and pedals for a day of sightseeing and enjoying the lush and verdurous vegetation, starting from Split to a different town heading south to Dubrovnik. They will ride anywhere from 20 to 40 miles stopping at designated areas for lunch and dinner. Their luggage will be transported for them each day and dropped off at the hotel where they will be spending the night. This is the first time Josefina and Rafael will be traveling with an organized tour. Normally, they would venture off by themselves when they vacationed abroad, but this time, Rafael had a frayed Achilles tendon, which has kept him from running for approximately nine months. Since they like to exercise daily, they decided to go on a biking vacation. On previous trips Rafael could run or swim when they were close to the ocean; then, they would continue their journey by renting a car or catching a train. They looked forward to this new adventure not having to worry about booking hotel rooms and thinking about where to eat.

As they sat down at the local coffee shop with their lattes in hand, they looked out the street window and began a gentle colloquy. People near them were hooked up to their iPads, computers, and smartphones. Soft music played in the background. They talked about work, family, hobbies, and political topics. Efraín had been in San Antonio now for twenty years. He emigrated from El Salvador after being harassed by gang members wanting him to join their *pandilla* (gang). They threatened to cut off his left hand with a machete if he didn't succumb to their request. His family owned a dry cleaning business in the capital of San Salvador, and they were coerced and extorted for rent by the gang members of the MS-13. They paid approximately $1,000.00 a month to keep their business open. He and his family, consisting of his parents and younger sister, hired a *coyote* to help them travel to the Texas border in 1999. They paid him $10,000.00 to transport them by bus and car to the boundary separating Mexico from Texas. They applied for asylum, and it was granted to them a year later. Luckily, some family members living in El Paso helped them with the required paperwork and lawyer fees. In addition, they had a place to stay in El Paso before moving to San Antonio and opening a dry cleaning business on North New Braunfels Avenue in the spring of 2001. It was an arduous and tiring process, but they were lucky compared to many who leave their hometowns in Central America and walk more than a thousand miles to reach the U.S. border to eventually be deported back to their countries. Many lost their lives or were victims of crimes along the long trek. It was disheartening to think about their plight.

It was difficult for Sasha, Josefina, and Rafael to fathom the journey taken by Efraín and the thousands of Central American immigrants now advancing in caravans with their families and small children to the U.S. and Mexican border. It is a crisis that affects refugees and immigrants not only from poverty-induced countries in Mexico, Latin America, and Africa but also from nations all over the world, especially in war-stricken areas in the Middle East. They asked themselves how does it affect the average American citizens like themselves who haven't experienced such hardships, and what is their responsibility? It's easy to dismiss the problems of distant countries that don't directly impact our daily lives. As friends they knew these issues needed to be discussed, and somehow it was their responsibility to have this discourse. The question remained. What could they do as they meditated on a maxim proclaimed by Ortega y Gasset, the Spanish essayist and philosopher? He affirmed in his writings, *"Somos ciudadanos del mundo"*. (We are citizens of the world.) As citizens of the world, what could they do directly or indirectly to extrapolate conclusively and possibly alleviate these negative ills influencing all countries as citizens of the world?

After enjoying a nice bike ride with approximately 900 cyclists during the San Antonio Wildflower Ride, Rafael and Josefina were surprised to read about another shooting at a Southern California synagogue that killed one 60-year-old woman and wounded Rabbi Yisroel Goldstein. Goldstein stated, "We are a Jewish nation that will stand tall. We will not let anyone take us down. Terrorism like this will not take us down." An eight-year-old girl along with her 34-year-old uncle were also wounded but released from the hospital. The attack came exactly six months after a mass shooting in a Pittsburgh synagogue. Luckily, the gunman's gun jammed, and he couldn't continue the inexplicable carnage.

John Earnest, 19 years old, was the attacker who posted a "manifesto" on his social media account. What is the cause of anti-Semitism or any other type of racism? John was a nursing student on the Dean's List where he attended college. He chose a profession in which he was going to care for people of all races. Is there an explanation for this heinous crime? Josefina knew we lived in a country of religious freedom, and each person has the right to pursue his/her dreams in a free and equitable society. Where does this despicable hate come from? This is the million-dollar question. Why attack worshippers at a synagogue who are going there to pray and worship God? God represents love, peace, tolerance, and equality for all people. He does not discriminate between one religious faith and another.

Rafael and his friends thought through these issues frequently as they gathered once a month at the local coffee house on Broadway St. He opined that it might be due to some extent to the isolation many feel from social media. If you look around most public places, whether it be in a restaurant, library, gym, or bus, people are plugged into their cell phones. They are engrossed looking at their device, listening to music, or posting comments on their Facebook or Instagram accounts. PlayStation and video games seem to dominate and control the attention of many. As a result, people are not dialoguing face to face with one another. This is a lost art in our society. Schools are still segregated for the most part since zip codes determine where children go to school. If a child lives in a wealthier neighborhood that pays higher property taxes, they will attend academic institutions with bigger budgets to pay for better qualified teachers. If a child grows up in a poorer neighborhood, which could be primarily a Hispanic or Black community, there will be scarcer economic resources to pay teachers and to provide better schools and educational opportunities for students. Furthermore, schoolchildren populations are less integrated because there is not a balanced mix of Whites, Blacks, Hispanics, and other ethnic groups.

This could be compounded by neighborhoods where Jewish, Muslims, and Christians are isolated from one another. This creates a toxic and volatile environment because children are sheltered from diversity; thus, they are not exposed to viewpoints that differ from their own. It's of "tectonic significance" for children to be exposed to dissimilar cultures and perspectives other than their own. This would probably help eliminate the abominable and bigoted groups that seem to be flourishing in our country and throughout the world. To assume that the White race is being eradicated by the influx of immigrants from Mexico, Central America, and Latin America is a mistake. We cannot blame our personal problems and lack of fulfillment on other people. Most immigrants, who migrate to the U.S., are willing to work hard to support their families. Hate groups do not adhere to the maxim, "Due unto others as you would have them do unto you." No racial or ethnic group here is trying to invade another.

Another topic surfaced during their shared coffee hour. It was an article written on May 6, 2019, "No U.S. Intervention in Venezuela" by Jovanni Reyes, a retired U.S. Army veteran who holds a master's degree in international relations. He believed Nicolás Maduro was elected democratically during the elections on May 20, 2018. Even though the election process was heavily guarded and monitored by people from the United States, Spain, Germany, South Africa, Russia, and various Latin American and Caribbean countries, Maduro supposedly won the elections. What Reyes seems to disregard is the fact that fraud did take place and has always taken place in countries like Venezuela, Guatemala, El Salvador, Nicaragua, Peru, and others. This is nothing new, but Reyes seems to overlook this point. The Venezuelan workers are given incentives to vote for the leftist regime, one founded by the late Hugo Chávez. Maybe homes are painted or extra money is donated to the poor and working class to gain their support. The rich and elite always benefit from a leftist regime since they are able to prosper from the Venezuelan oil and make investments overseas. Manuel, one of Rafael's friends, believes economic sanctions from the U.S. and other countries are justified to demand another election. Guaidó, the opposition leader, may be the right choice for Venezuela. He seems to be supported by the working class as well as some of the elites who are willing to take a stand against Maduro. The question becomes: Why doesn't the Maduro regime allow humanitarian aid to reach those who are starving in a country that is suffering economically? Maduro should be concerned about the well-being of his people. If the majority of Venezuelans supported him, why are they leaving the country by the hundreds every day?

Manuel and his friends are not suggesting a military intervention by the U.S. or any other country at this point. A revolution may eventually develop against the regime in the months to come. The international community should focus on creating commissions of anti-corruption and anti-fraud, not only in the presidential elections of Venezuela but also in all the agencies of this country. The police, military, and all elected officials must be overseen and accounted for in aiding a dictatorship that conceals its identity under the veil of democracy while it steals from the poor and middle class to fill its own pockets with riches. This is a chronic problem embedded in the Venezuelan cultural fabric since the colonial invasion of the Spaniards in the 16th century and the ensuing dictatorship of Bolívar who espoused the unification of Colombia, Venezuela, and Panama in the 19th century. This democratic concept of "unification" was a disguise to impose his military and political power to become the sole dictator of Venezuela during the revolution against Spain, which ended in 1821. These are some of the issues that must be considered when studying and commenting on the current events in Venezuela.

It's easy to take a liberal stance of nonintervention like Reyes suggests or a conservative position of a military invasion by some in Congress and the Trump administration. Josefina and her friends concurred it is more effective to take a middle-ground approach by maintaining economic sanctions but avoiding a military stance unless a country like Russia becomes involved militarily. But, more urgently, these commissions against corruption and fraud must be the centerpiece of these discussions. They must be pursued and conferred at the highest political levels. Rafael did not think U.S. universities and their international programs were effective in this area since the majority of universities are very liberal and advocate no type of intervention at all. This is evident in Reyes's viewpoint regarding the current Venezuelan crisis.

Rafael savored his cup of coffee and the moment shared with his friends as he reminisced about a recent trip he took to Valley View, about 60 miles north of Dallas, to participate in the Texasman Triathlon at the Ray Roberts Lake a few weeks ago. He was amazed by the amount of traffic travelling up and down the IH-35 corridor joining San Antonio, Austin, Killeen, Waco, and Dallas. It was a circus of metal vehicles moving on rubber tires filling his view for miles on end. It was a ceaseless stream of motion storming along the massive masterpiece of architectural structures, folding toll roads, and endless highways as they pierced towards the sky. Roads were interwoven in all directions creating a mural of creative art with artists standing in every direction with paint brushes in their hands. The imaginary figures crafted sparse fields of wildflowers with a sea of chapels in Waco, restaurants, establishments, and gigantic glass structures housing banks, trade centers, insurance and medical companies, and other behemoths of a free democracy. It was a panorama that seemed to compound itself each and every year.

SIMÓN BOLÍVAR

RAFAEL KNEW IT was quintessential to return to broaching the topic of "infamous figure" of Simón Bolívar, known as *El Liberador* (The Liberator) of Venezuela and Colombia, in the War of Independence from Spain that began in Hidalgo, Mexico in 1810 and spread across Latin America until its conclusion in 1821. Bolívar was inspired by the French Revolution of 1879 and the American Revolution of 1776. He was born in Venezuela, grew up in an elite Creole family, and received a traditional Latin American education. He visited Spain and France and was inspired primarily by Swiss and French thinkers, like Rousseau and Montesquieu, during the Enlightenment or Age of Reason. He believed in a united Latin America but was more of a pragmatist. He was able to unite the Black *llaneros* in Venezuela and Colombia to join his military to defeat the remaining Spanish troops in Latin America. Spain was losing its power and presence in the New World after Napoleon invaded its borders in 1808, and when the English Royal Navy defeated the Spanish Armada (naval fleet) earlier in 1588.

Bolívar succeeded in unifying Venezuela, Colombia, and part of Ecuador. However, the fighting among the elite and factions of Blacks and poorer Creoles continued. In addition, Bolívar believed in effectuating a strong centralist government controlled by the military. He also thought it was necessary for a president, himself in this case, to remain in power for life. Contradictorily, he advocated for the sovereignty of all people and for the rule of law. In the chaos of establishing a new Latin American nation, the economy never developed. Latin America was dependent on imports received from Britain, the U.S., and other European countries. There were no investments directed towards agriculture and manufacturing. Land grants given to soldiers, who fought during the revolution, were mostly sold for cash. The economic and social conditions of Latin American remained in a state of disarray.

Bolívar is probably best known for writing *La carta de Jamaica* in September 1815. He was in exile in Jamaica after a military defeat in Latin America. In this essay he developed his ideas of a unified Latin America and Gran Colombia, comprising the countries of Venezuela, Colombia, Ecuador, and Panama. He espoused the ideas of Montesquieu, the French writer and philosopher, who was against the control of the monarchy in favor of a society representative of all its people with a government elected by the people. Simón also supported the conceptional design of *mestizaje*, the mixing of ethnic races. Latin America could no longer existentially sustain the cultural, political, and economical racial Divide between *peninsulares* (Spaniards), the *criollos* (inhabitants born in Latin America), Blacks, and the Indigenous populations. All ethnic groups are extremely momentous and there should no longer be a barrier separating races. A synchronistic approach for joining races, politics, and job opportunities should apply to all citizens of Latin America.

LATIN AMERICA AND BENITO JUÁREZ

ACCORDING TO MARCOS, Rafael, and his friends this was the primary downfall of Latin America then and now. This meshing of the races did not occur then, and it is still a "troubling obstacle" today creating instability in these countries. This has added fuel to the fire of immigration as we witness thousands of immigrants leaving Venezuela, Guatemala, Honduras, Mexico, and many other countries around the globe on a weekly basis trekking to the U.S. border or other countries in search of a slight ray of hope for better jobs and desirable living conditions. It is necessary to consider the political ideas of Montesquieu, the 18th century French thinker, who wrote the *Spirit of Laws* (1750). In his book he stressed the utmost relevance of the separation of power between the executive, legislative, and judiciary branches of government; thus, ending the feudal system of France and other European countries where the haughty and avaricious state ruthlessly partitioned leverage between the monarchy, aristocracy, and common people. The United States and many European countries adopted Montesquieu's political model, which relied on the laws and checks and balances created by each government.

Unfortunately, many countries in Latin America and other Third World countries, like Africa, may conceal themselves under the Montesquieu cloak of liberal and equitable government, but they are still riddled by oppressive and corrupt governments in which the elite increase their wealth, and the poor sink further and further into poverty. This is evident when examining the history of Mexico in which the Partido Revolucionario Institucional (PRI) has ruled since the end of the Mexican Revolution in 1921. The party has disguised itself by stating it is a democracy encompassed and structured around the three branches of government: the executive, legislative, and judiciary. However, fraud and malfeasance have triumphed in all these administrative levels, in which officials are not appointed in free elections by the people, but by the elite who control the money and authority. These elements of injustice are corrosive and divisive.

It is *de rigueur* (indispensable) to examine the utmost relevance of Benito Juárez, the first Indigenous president, to govern Mexico in the midnineteenth century. Juárez was born in 1806 in San Pablo Guelatao, Oaxaca, Mexico to a poor Zapotec Indigenous family. Both of his parents died when he was three years, and he and his two sisters, María Josefa and Rosa, lived with their grandparents for a while. Unfortunately, his *abuelos* also deceased so he ended up moving in with his uncle, Bernardino Juárez, who taught him Spanish since Benito only spoke Zapotec, an Indigenous dialect.

At the age of 12, he left San Pablo Guelatao to go to Oaxaca. Some say his uncle didn't take care of him, and Benito grew tired of herding and attending to sheep. However, it is strongly believed he left because he was enthralled in learning about the world outside of his small village *a lo* José Ortega y Gasset, the renown Spanish author and philosopher of the late 19th and early 20th century, who advocated for all people to become *ciudadanos del mundo* (world citizens).

Gasset implied it was wrong for individuals to isolate themselves in their familiar town or city to become insulated from the "exterior global community" as they singularly reside only in their small cultural circle of residence, church, family, and familiar acquaintances who all speak the same language, whether it be English or French, for instance.

It is easy to form false beliefs fomenting bigotry, prejudice, and hatred for any circle of people or foreigners unlike themselves—for instance—who also speak an alien language and have dissimilar cultural traditions and skin color. Not becoming *citoyens du monde* (global citizens) is extremely perilous because of the acutely severe racism and hatred it breeds.

Benito stayed in Oaxaca where his sister, Josefa, was working at the home of Mr. and Mrs. Maza. There, she introduced him to Mr. Antonio Salanueva, a priest of the Third Order of San Francisco who was also a bookbinder. Mr. Salanueva helped him enroll in the Seminario de Santa Cruz where Benito excelled as a student. Benito abandoned his studies to become a priest and matriculated in the Instituto de Ciencias y Artes de Oaxaca where he obtained his law degree in 1834. At this time, he sympathized with the Liberals in Mexico.

The political, social, and economic conditions of Mexico after the War of Independence in 1821 were fragmented. The vast amounts of land were controlled by a few, poverty was rampant everywhere due to the many years of foreign invasions, and the illiteracy rate was at 80%. The Catholic Church controlled much of the wealth of the country, and there was not a viable system of communication between the towns. Furthermore, the country was sparsely populated. After becoming the Minister of Justice, Benito created and mandated the *Ley de Juárez* on the 25 of November 1855, which granted the separation of state and church. This was extremely important since the Catholic Church imposed mandatory tithes on the population and owned most of the land. The Church demanded that everyone had to be a Catholic, and the law did not allow for anyone to belong to another religious denomination. A law was also ratified and approved to allow civil weddings in 1859 in which couples could choose to marry outside of the regulations and confines of the Church. Births, deaths, weddings, and divorces were now administered and recorded in civil registries. Education was now provided to all citizens of Mexico free of cost and without any religious connotations or obligations. Juárez believed free nations must be comprised of educated people.

Sadly, the Conservatives (members of the Church and military) did not concede to these laws, which resulted in *La Guerra de Reforma* (Reform War) from December 1858 until December 1860. The Liberals won, and Benito Juárez became president in 1861. Interestingly, Mexico suffered from a financial crisis due to the war, and the government put a stop to paying its foreign debt, which caused the French to invade and go to war with Mexico from 1862-1868. Rafael concluded that these events led to a conflict between Liberals and Conservatives affecting the poor who belonged to neither side. It boils down today to the haves and have-nots, plain and simple. But, curiously enough, Benito Juárez was the only mestizo to ever rise from a modest upbringing to be elected as the president of Mexico. Unfortunately, the "puzzling but disturbing ethnic-race argument" today is one that influences politics not only in Mexico but in most countries of the world.

CROATIA AND PUERTO RICO

RAFAEL AND JOSEFINA had just returned from a two-week vacation to Croatia with a bike tour organized by Backroads. They had a wonderful time biking with 20 other people from the *pueblo*, beginning in Split and ending in Dubrovnik. The deep blue Adriatic Sea was truly beautiful and refreshing to watch from the wake of the sailboat that took them to three disparate islands on their tour: Hvar, Korcula, and Brac. What was fascinating about Croatia was its long and diverse history. The people who lived in Croatia date back to 5000 BC, and they learned to farm although they only had stone tools. Later, they acquired bronze and iron. After 390 BC, the Greeks established colonies along the Dalmatian Coast. It wasn't until 299 BC that the Roman Empire took control of parts of Croatia, and they ruled all of Croatia by 12 AD. The Romans divided Croatia into provinces: the Dalmatian Coast, Noricum (which included parts of Austria), and Pannonia (which comprised parts of present-day Hungary). Roman control of Croatia came to an end in the 5th century.

It is regarded by archaeologists that the Croatian culture consists of the Slavs who are Indo-European and began to migrate and populate Croatia in the 7th century. Some considered them to be nomads who established themselves in the mountainous and forest-like regions, and others surmised they originated in Western and Southern Russia and parts of Iran. These nomads attacked the Romans, and they joined the Avar Clans to help them fight the commanding Romans. In the 9th century, Croatia became a part of the Western Catholic Church based in Rome instead of the Eastern Orthodox Church founded in Constantinople. In the 11th century King Petar Kresimir united the separate territorial domains of the Croatian states that had been established on the coast and inland. However, at the beginning of the 12th century, King Koloman of Hungary conquered Croatia. Trade flourished at this time in Croatia, and *la vie quotidienne en ville* (daily town life) was also invigorated.

Rafael was fascinated by Croatia, especially Dubrovnik, formerly known as Ragusa, which the refugees from Epidaurus (known today as Cavtat) founded in the 7th century. Dubrovnik was ruled over the centuries by the Ostrogothic, Byzantine, and Venetian Empires; it acquired a certain autonomy from the Hungarian Kingdom in 1358. Until 1808 Ragusa was a free city-state even though it paid annual amends to the Ottoman Empire to retain its independence over several centuries. Ragusa reached its economic and cultural peak in the 15th and 16th centuries after forming an alliance with Ancona, a strong maritime country in the Adriatic, which kept the Venetians from dominating this part of the sea. This alliance allowed Ragusa and Ancona to expand their own trade route.

Dubrovnik forged a successful scheme for a huge fleet of merchant ships known for its dazzling ability to navigate to numerous ports. Their free-seafaring trade and skilled diplomacy contributed greatly to their economic wealth. In the 15th century, Dubrovnik exported soap, glass, and cloths, which were their own manufactured goods. It was also involved in the commutation of exchanging livestock, agricultural, and mining goods. It launched its own colony in India where one can still find evidence of its significant political power with the Church of St. Blaise, the patron saint of Dubrovnik, which is still standing. The invaluable-significant "paramountcy" of the Republic declined after the discovery of America in 1492 when trade routes transferred primarily to the Atlantic. Dubrovnik was also devastated by a powerful earthquake and a tsunami that shattered the city and killed many of its inhabitants in 1667.

Josefina and Rafael walked along the walls that surrounded Dubrovnik on May 29, 2019, soaking in the beauty of the vistas of the deep azure of the blue Adriatic Sea. They made a connection between this Croatian city, known as the pearl of the Adriatic, and the city of San Juan, Puerto Rico. Puerto Rico was known as *La Perla* (the Pearl) of the Caribbean, centered strategically at the cusp of the Caribbean and Atlantic Ocean, joining the trade routes between Mexico, Latin America, and European countries from the 15th through the 18th centuries. As a child Rafael remembered visiting *El Morro*, the incredibly massive fort with its walls protecting Old San Juan. It was built by the Spaniards as a safe haven for Spanish galleons to rest before traversing the Atlantic with ships full of gold and silver on its treacherous voyage back to Spain. Lurking behind the waves of this idyllic island, history reminds us of the dangers posed by the "phantasmagoric phantoms" of Sir Francis Drake, John Hawkins, and other pirates lingering to attack and plunder the Spanish vessels.

Rafael roamed the interior of *El Morro*, which means a promontory, a point of highland that jets out into a large body of water. This position was crucial for protecting the bay and island from invaders. King Charles V of Spain authorized the Spanish fort or the Castillo San Felipe del Morro to be built in 1539, and engineers designed the original structure in 1589. However, *El Morro*, that people visit today, took more than 200 years to complete. It contains a maze of dungeons, storage areas, and passageways, which mysteriously reveal this significant historical period. The fort represents a bridge between the Old and New Worlds. It's a place where one can enter one of the *garitas*, small turrets, located at several key positions on the upper level of the fort and look over the ominous but beautiful sea to ponder Puerto Rico's panorama of the past and present. It's a place where poets can imagine and compose the perfect metaphor within a poem. It's a place where Rafael could return to in his mind to search for the existential meaning of life and place it in a jar of clay. Many times, one sees and experiences these moments, visiting places like *El Morro* and Dubrovnik, to only capture a snapshot of their immense significance in the wider spectrum of one's existence.

This is why it becomes necessary for Rafael to write about his experience and to share it with Josefina to reflect and digest the power and privilege of travelling and processing these insights to make them relevant to one's own life. One realizes that he or she is not a separate microscopic piece of the world, which remains separate from its macroscopic entity, but that one forms an intricate part of this global reality. Without reflection it is impossible to conceive of this connection between cultures and the historical facts of centuries preceding our modern age. Rafael and Josefina agreed that it's fundamental to partake in the arduous task of delving into history and visiting these historical sites without understanding completely their relevance. In the search for meaning after some research, one can grasp the connectivity between all of humanity. Without this inquiry, it is impossible to see beyond our individual caves described by Plato in which our perspective of the world is not augmented unless we leave our original dwellings to explore beyond their borders.

AMERICAN TERROR, INTERPRETING, AND ISOLATION

THIS MORNING RAFAEL woke up and was stunned to read about another lone gunman who created havoc by shooting rounds of bullets from an assault weapon outside the Earle Cabell Federal Building in Dallas, Texas on June 17, 2019. Luckily, no one was shot or injured other than the lone gunman, Brian Isaack Clyde who was 22 years old. He served as an infantryman in the Army from 2015 to 2017 but was discharged as a private first class in 2017. He had recently graduated with an associate degree of applied science from Del Mar College, a Corpus Christi community college. He was shot by officers amidst shattering panes of glass from a revolving door of the federal building. After being taken to the hospital, he died shortly afterwards. Officials are still trying to piece together a motive for his actions.

Rafael, Josefina, and their friends often pondered the question: Why are there so many random acts of terror and violence in our country and throughout the world? Where is society failing? Why are so many gunmen so young? These are important issues to discuss, and many times we, as a society, ignore them since it is much easier to bury them than to try to find a cause and solution. Josefina believed "failure" comes to mind as she contemplated this crisis in American society. We, as individuals and a society, have trouble dealing with defeat. If this young man was discharged from the U.S. Army for some kind of flop or mental illness, the stigma remains with this person for the rest of his life. Unfortunately, we all fail at some point in our lives, and we will continue to flounder throughout the course of our *vidas* (lives). Josefina remembered discussing on numerous occasions with Rafael the countless times he had taken the oral exam for court interpreters, and the many times he had failed it. He had come up short at least four or five times, but he continues to study for it. Rafael will take it again this August, and there is a possibility he might fail it again. Sure it bothered him that he had missed the mark by not passing this exam many times. However, it has given him a chance to reflect and realize that people are not always successful in every endeavor they pursue.

The exam is comprised of three sections: sight translation, consecutive, and simultaneous. For the sight translation, one reads a legal document in Spanish and translates it to English. Then, one reads another document in English and translates it to Spanish. For the consecutive portion, a person listens to a lawyer questioning a witness or defendant in court and interprets from English to Spanish and from Spanish to English. Finally, for the simultaneous section, one interprets the introductory remarks or verdict of a judge or a lawyer's statement from English to Spanish. This is done simultaneously, meaning, it is interpreted at a fast pace into Spanish, a second or two behind the speaker who is speaking in English. The exam is challenging because the test-taker must know all the judicial vocabulary and the many themes that pertain to legal matters, whether they be criminal or civil, for example. A person also must have the mental agility to remember facts and information and to transcribe idiomatic expressions that don't translate literally between languages.

Rafael has learned that he likes the idea of court interpreting, but he realizes that he does not enjoy studying for the exam. He has a set of CDs for practicing the three modes of the exam with a variety of courtroom and legal situations. He realizes that he still hasn't mastered many of the legal jargon and vocabulary, which are deciphering linguistically, accurately, and precisely in an instance. Since he likes to create by writing poetry and fiction, it is difficult for him to interpret and repeat concepts and events as they happened. It is repetitive and does not require much critical thinking other than developing the mental agility for speed and exact verbal clarification. In addition, he is semiretired and has been busy lexically decoding for schools and medical clinics as an interpreter for Worldwide Languages. It is a small company in San Antonio, Texas that also offers language classes and translation services throughout the city *pour toutes les langues du monde* (for all the languages of the world). An interpreter does not have to be certified to work in these areas. Rafael qualified by presenting his documentation as a certified Spanish teacher and a recipient of a Master of Liberal Arts in Spanish literature with a minor in French literature.

His failure bothers him, but at the same time, it has given him something to do along with his other hobbies: training for triathlons, travelling, writing poetry and fiction, and interpreting part-time. If he were to pass the oral exam, he wonders if he would enjoy this profession in court since it would be more time consuming than the work he does now. For example, when he is assigned to interpret at a school or health clinic, he only works for an hour or two at the most. Being in a courtroom setting might involve analyzing and decoding legal jargon for exegesis for five or six hours a day depending on the case. Rafael struggles with this type of commitment at this period of his life in which he is semiretired. At the same time, he can strive for this goal even though he knows he is not completely passionate about becoming a court interpreter.

As he shares his thoughts with Josefina and his friends, Rafael wonders if he could be content with not preparing to become a court interpreter. Should he keep trying or stop after making several attempts to pass the oral exam? Could he be satisfied with just doing what he is doing with his writings, triathlons, reading, and travelling? These are questions we all grapple with as we enter retirement and divergent phases of our lives. It is exciting, but, at the same time, it can also be a period that causes some anxiety. This is a normal part of the human condition. Rafael thinks of people who reach retirement, and it seems like they don't do much other than the usual things we all do: eat, sleep, take care of their homes and themselves, visit with friends or family, for instance. These are good things to do, but shouldn't there be more to life? Shouldn't we, as individuals, spawn and conceive something authentic? Although Rafael is not a professional writer, he feels it's essential to inscribe and observe the world because this allows him to participate and to reflect upon the events around him. It provides a certain type of *le sens* and significance for him individually. Yes, it would be great for others to read his work, but this would require a lot of time and money spent marketing his books. This might be something he pursues later, but for now, it seems like a commitment he is not willing to invest his time doing.

Pedro, one of his friends, who he had not seen in a long time asked him: "So what does this soliloquy on failure have to do with the young gunman, Brian Isaack Clyde, who tried to kill others in the recent terror attack in Dallas?" Pedro believed it was related to the constant isolation we all face in society. Our phones insulate us from one another, and the media bombards us from our "idiotic boxes" at home, leaving us with an overwhelming sense of being alone. When we go to the gym, for example, to work out, we are plugged into our phones and don't even look and acknowledge the person next to us. At grocery stores we push our carts along aisles filling our baskets with food and other necessities without greeting others passing by us. Of course, from time to time, we greet one another, but it is not the norm. Pedro thinks of his father, now in his mid-eighties, who only watches TV when he enters his home. As soon as he enters the door, he goes for the remote to click on the box. It is on while he changes clothes, naps, and eats. Media becomes an illusionary friend and companion. Pedro believed that young adults as well as grownups and senior citizens are affected by isolation.

Rafael agreed with Pedro that much of our time is spent alone. It must have to do with our culture of self-reliance espoused by Ralph Waldo Emerson, the great American writer of the 19th century. He was one of the Romantic's like Henry David Thoreau who recommended we *bailamos* (dance) and frolic aimlessly from time-to-time *en la soledad* (in solitude) and nature contemplating life and its meaning. However, today we seem to meander less outdoors in nature and spend more time staring blankly into our TVs, phones, and computer screens. Rafael often thought about the detachment he feels at church services where sermons and traditions are monotonous and repetitive. He often pondered to himself: "What is the purpose of going to churches in which services are ceaselessly "worthless" with no ripe fruit and lack substance?" We are all subject to the mundane and endless boredom of life. Rafael many times catches himself sitting in front of the *caja idiótica* (idiot box-TV) after dinner surfing through the "waves" of channels looking for something informative and substantial to watch. It keeps us from doing some other activity. Rafael, as most people, feel like they always need to be doing something productive, whether it is chores, yard work, exercising, organizing a closet, or going to the grocery store. These are the everyday activities that consume us.

UNCLE ROBERT

THE KEY TO life is the ability to establish a spiritual harmony with the things we do and encounter daily. It is something we must attempt to pursue regularly. It's about balancing and rebalancing each day as one navigates the distractions, failures, and successes we all experience. Rafael knew it was necessary to have these discussions with oneself and others when possible. Writing provides the catharsis for having this dialogue and interaction with oneself because one can see thoughts printed on a page. His impressions shifted to a poem he recently wrote dedicated to Robert, Josefina's uncle, who recently passed away. Rafael wanted to include the poem below:

"Robert"

The ocean's breath
roars in the background,
A house full of family
rejoicing in fellowship,

A quiet and gentle disposition
fills the upper sunroom
of the third floor,
Four chairs sit steadily,
A table sustaining a puzzle,
Robert meticulously places
one piece after another
in its appropriate place...

I remember his kindness,
His dedication caring for his ill wife,
Like the lonely seagull soaring
over whitecaps to join its flock on the sand,
Robert loved to sit with his bowl of cereal or hot soup
amongst his brother, sisters, daughters,
and other family members...

His joyful and clear eyes always
revealed his faith, joy, and childlike ways,
His cotton shirt, pants, and high-top
Converse tennis shoes matched
his love for orderliness,
The way he bit into the large
chocolate chip cookie,
Bite by bite he savored each piece,
We relished each moment with Robert...

We'll miss him as we put
the pieces of our life's puzzle
together with his spirit nearby,
We'll miss his steady hand and sense
of humor playing cards,
We'll smile knowing his presence
remains in our hearts,
Upon returning to Nags Head,
I'll look out the windows of the beach house,
I'll see Robert sitting in God's embrace
savoring a golden chocolate chip
cookie together in the clouds
overlooking the sea.

Poetry allows the poet to encapsulate a few images to remind him of people he cherishes. These depictions live in his memories as he recalls that person and relives those moments shared with him. It is a creative outlet for the muse allowing him to mourn and keep the deceased person's presence alive in his consciousness.

Josefina and Rafael sat at their copious dining room table in the back sunroom of their home in San Antonio sipping steaming green tea from their mugs. Josefina remembered her uncle, Robert, playing cards and socializing with other family members every November in Nags Head, North Carolina. She cried after reading Rafael's poem dedicated to her uncle. The yearly family reunion was a wonderful way to connect with family and to enjoy watching each other growing old. There was something majestic and memorable about sitting at the beach house overlooking the wild Atlantic Ocean in the background. Its movement reminded Josefina of the quick "paramountcy" of time from one year to the next. She reminisced about her mother, Joanna, who passed away about four years ago. Josefina recalled the agony Joanna experience after tumbling down some steps and fracturing her hip. She rode in an ambulance back to Norfolk, Virginia accompanying her mother to a hospital to prepare her for surgery. It was a memory that surfaced from time to time as she sauntered along the beach with its lapping *petit olitas* (little waves) to the pier a mile away with her sister Anastasia. It was the same pier Joanna used to amble to with them in the past.

THE CATHARSIS OF WRITING

WRITING IS ONE of the few creative outlets for recording one's thoughts directly on paper. It serves the same purpose as a diary for expressing one's emotions and memories. The pages are filled with reactions, opinions, intellectual musings, and other creative rants. It's filling "jars of clay" with food, knickknacks, pens, or ideas. It is insignificant if one writes novels, essays, works of nonfiction, poetry, and essays. It avowed Rafael the time to meditate and *escudriñar* (examine) his surroundings. It provides a chance to discipline the mind to focus on: the clicking of a fan above, the humming of a refrigerator, the movement of leaves swaying in the air, the lazy white and grey cat, Garmo, napping on the outdoor-deck table, the world at large, and the steadiness of the huge pecan tree outside viewed from the window inside. Writing on a *página* (page) is like taking a stone and throwing it in a calm lake. One witnesses the concentric circles in the water flowing and cresting in unison. Words flow, ideas are formed, and philosophies are created.

Rafael thought about his experience this morning at the gym Crunch. Today he started off with the incline bench press doing his first set of ten with 135 lbs. Between sets he used a 25 lb. weight to do 50 abdominal twists with 20 lateral extensions on each side. Almost everyone was tuned into their phones listening to music. Rafael rarely had a conversation with anyone, and there were certain people he had seen there for approximately two years with whom he had never spoken to or even had eye contact with. On his second set of inclines, he benched 155 lbs. for eight repetitions. For his third set he pushed 165 for six repetitions; then, he pressed 175 for four reps. Finally, he lifted 185 lbs. for two repetitions. He asked a young Black man if he could give him a spot on his last two sets. This helped Rafael in case he was not able to lift the weight by himself. Rafael also assisted him with two of his lifts. They were cordial to each and thanked one another for each other's help. Other than a brief exchange of words, Rafael normally did not speak to others; it was common for most members not to speak with each other.

Yes, people come to the gym to work out, but it just seemed strange that people would not talk to each other more. Rafael wondered if mankind was losing the ability to speak to one another. Was it inconvenient? Was it a waste of time? He recently sent a message to his sister-in-law regarding an issue pertaining to her son. He and Josefina were both concerned about her son, a young adolescent. But his sister-in-law chose not to respond to his message. Isn't it common courtesy to respond to each other, especially when one's intention is to help and to provide a respective viewpoint? Many are set in their own ideologies, whether they are political, religious, or personal. The inflexibility to dialogue and to carry on a conversation with someone who holds a contrasting perspective is commonplace today, it seems. Rafael is also reminded of an aunt who doesn't respond or reciprocate to Christmas and birthday cards he sends her. ¿Por qué? Is the pain of a past occurrence so deep that it keeps one from forgiving and moving on? Are humans so busy they can't respond to others, even family members? It's a weird phenomenon, but it appears to be *quotidian*.

For this reason, it's essential to frame with words on paper or to make jars with clay. *Travail* (Work) without words to reflect, play without a creative outlet, relationships without meaningful conversations, and physical training without a purpose leave one aimlessly meandering from activity to activity without direction and value. Attending a medical ceremony for fellows completing and graduating from their two-year residency program, where some guests don't greet each other after years of being acquainted, is odd and uncomfortable. Why? The human touch is lost in our modern-day society. Even doctors who care for unknown patients, lack the ability to greet and be cordial to people they know. Why? These are the questions Rafael enjoyed asking and trying to answer with Josefina and his other friends. Love is the answer, but it is so difficult to achieve.

It seems like fear predominates and spawns division between people; therefore, we, as humans, are fragile. We are like "jars of clay" that shatter when dropped. We forever need to pick up the pieces and glue them back together. This is what God does for us on a daily basis.

IRAN AND AMERICAN SOCCER

AS RAFAEL BEGAN his day with a warm cup of cappuccino, he reflected on the recent affairs between Iran and Trump. Marc A. Thiessen actually gave President Trump a high grade with dealing with Iran and its Supreme Leader Ayatollah Ali Khamenei in his article, "Trump succeeding where Obama failed" from June 28, 2019 in the *San Antonio Express-News*. The U.S. has tightened sanctions on Iran after pulling out of the nuclear arms deal established by Barack Obama during his administration. The sanctions have hurt Iran in that oil exports have dropped from 2.5 million barrels per day in April 2018 to just 300,000 barrels per day this month. The U.S. State Department indicates that oil sanctions alone will deny the regime $50 billion in revenue, or 40 percent of Iran's annual budget. Trump's campaign has directly caused inflation to spiral, and Iran has been forced to cut funds to terrorist groups like Hezbollah and Hamas. The Iranian military and the Islamic Revolutionary Guard Corps have also suffered. Trump aborted a military strike on Iran after it downed a U.S. military drone supposedly flying in their air space. No one was killed, but if Trump wouldn't have aborted a military strike on key Iranian military areas at least 150 Iranians would have died. It was the right decision by Trump for his administration not to strike militarily and to further tighten the already existing economic sanctions.

What perplexes Rafael and Josefina is that the Liberals cannot give credit to this accomplishment by Trump. They accuse him of not enforcing the "red line" in this case as Obama had proposed in Syria after the Middle Eastern regime used chemical weapons against its population, killing many women, men, and children. Obama did not strike militarily, but Trump did after the Syrian government continued to use chemical weapons upon civilians. No country wants to go to war, but countries like Iran and Syria must be confronted with a strong hand since they support terrorism and nuclear arms escalation. It is understandable that President Trump is an irascible character, but Liberals and Conservatives need to learn to come together even though they disagree on many issues. This is a major problem in American politics, and the vast divisiveness has caused a rift that seems almost irreparable. In Rafael's mind a strong third party in American politics needs to evolve, one that embraces both liberal and conservative values. A different mindset needs to surface in which members of divergent political parties learn to become more amicable towards each other. Capitalism and special interest groups in Washington influence many of the policies and laws created and ratified by the U.S. government. As a result, big businesses and corporations dictate the major issues pertaining to health care, military spending, taxation, and others. This aspect of capitalism needs to be modified and changed.

Josefina perused the morning paper and read an article about Megan Rapinoe who scored two goals to defeat France in their quarterfinal soccer match at the Women's World Cup in Paris this past week. Rapinoe is gay and is in a relationship with Sue Bird, a star with the Women's National Basketball Association. Rapinoe said she would not visit the White House if the team won or lost the WWC even after Trump invited the team to do so. Two years ago she knelt during the national anthem, showing her support and solidarity with Colin Kaepernick, the former San Francisco 49ers quarterback, who knelt during the anthem to call attention to racial inequality. The U.S. Soccer Federation adapted a rule that all players must stand during anthems. She has abided by this rule, but she has not sung or placed her hand over her heart during the U.S. anthem.

Rapinoe along with the other women-soccer players are also disputing the disparity in pay established by the International Federation of Association Football (FIFA) for paying men more than women. The winners of the men's World Cup in Russia were awarded $38 Million while the winners of the women's WC this year were awarded $4 million.

What has Rapinoe forgotten to recognize? She wouldn't be a soccer star if it were not for the opportunities to play she was afforded in the U.S. Her ability to protest and voice her views as a gay activist could only be accomplished in the U.S. If Rapinoe is so disgusted with President Trump and the racial disparity in the U.S., why doesn't she move to another country? There is no equal to the freedoms and opportunities Americans are granted in the U.S. even under the contentious leadership of President Trump. Gays and lesbians in other countries, like Brazil and Africa, for example, would not have the freedom and platform to celebrate and voice their rights during Pride month. In many countries of the world, gays and lesbians would be incarcerated. The freedoms gays and lesbians enjoy could only be accomplished in America. The landmark of the LGBT community began on June 28, 1969 with the Stonewall riots in Manhattan, New York City during a violent police raid on the LGBT community.

It just so happened Rapinoe scored two goals for the U.S. on June 28, 2019 in Paris to help the American team beat France to move on to the semifinal match with England in a couple of days. The U.S. women may complain about the disparity between salaries between men and women's soccer, but they surely get paid more or the same as other men's teams in the World Soccer League. However, only in the United States can women protest and voice their opinions, and actions will be set in place to hear them and promote change. According to Josefina, by not standing, singing, and placing your hand over your heart during the national anthem, you offend all Americans and the sacrifices they've made for the freedoms we as Americans enjoy. Rabinoe offends those Americans who support the LGBT community, and this should be noted. Her actions represent a disregard for our country, and she is abusing the privilege she has, as a renowned soccer player, to voice and stage her personal and political convictions. There is a place and time to do this, but it should not be on the soccer field programed for the world to view. Americans are individuals, and they can obviously choose how to live their lives. These are the freedoms they exercise and should preserve. But, by *la desestimación de su país* (scorning) their country and national anthem, they are proposing that the beacon of freedom, which is the U.S., should be disrespected and nullified. To do this is to return to the Stone Age and to strip the LGBT community and others from what Albert Camus, the French philosopher, affirms: *"C'est cela l'amour, tout donner, tout scrifier sans espoir de retour."*

"That is love, to give away everything, to sacrifice everything without the slightest desire to get anything in return." Their American forefathers endured many hardships so that we as U.S. citizens can live and cohabitate in a free democratic society in which we can vote and voice our opinions. Unwittingly, Rapinoe has moved our country back ten steps by her antics. Josefina's question remains: Is she aware of the disservice she has done to the LGBT community? Her intellectual high stance is a representation of a young infant in diapers still sucking her pacifier on a world stage, which is the opposite of what her intent was.

Rafael opined that many times Americans and other people from other countries, of course, base their convictions on the limitations imposed on them from their culture. In the U.S. Americans have the freedom to criticize the government and other institutions, but sometimes these liberties can be taken too far. Americans must contemplate all the opportunities they have at their disposal. Children, for example, have the space and the facilities to develop as young athletes. Most American children are not burdened by hunger and war destroying their country. They are not forced to immigrate to other countries due to corrupt police officers and gangs swarming and controlling the streets in their neighborhoods, as we are witnessing now with the flow of Central American immigrants to the U.S. and the southern and northern Mexican borders. This is a serious issue, and it is one we should all embrace. It seems like Rapinoe and other players and celebrities should use their popularity to address these issues. Maybe the soccer community could work with the U.S. and European governments to invest in these poor Central American communities to help children, boys and girls, carve out the space, equipment, and safety to play soccer and other sports. Instead of focusing so much on the disparity in pay between men and women athletes, there could be a focus on helping the poor of third-world countries to mature into young talented adolescent athletes with the dream of becoming professional athletes who could represent their countries on the world platform and give to others around the world.

FAMILY DYNAMICS AND THE ART OF CONVERSATIONS

AS RAFAEL THOUGHT about this topic along with other "profound ruminations," his mind returned to the comforting clicking of the fan in the yellow sunroom where he sat looking out the stain glassed window into the panorama of a green canvas, meditating as the hot sun dropped at the near dusk hour. He and Josefina had just returned from a trip to Abita Springs in Louisiana where they celebrated with other family members the 60th wedding anniversary of Josefina's Uncle Enrique and Auntie Francisca. They pondered the family dynamics of a dinner party at a refurbished plantation home converted into a restaurant. The art of a conversation surfaced as Josefina and Rafael "fully intuited;" *il se souvenait* (he remembered) the interactions between family members. It was interesting to note that many Millennials, several nieces and nephews, were inept at carrying on a conversation. They normally would remain silent unless one asked them a question. Rafael asked Manolo, Josefina's nephew: "So, how was your trip to Japan?" Manolo responded: "It was great! We visited many Japanese gardens, ate wonderful food, and visited the Hiroshima Peace Memorial. We really enjoyed it. It was interesting to observe how the Japanese greet and bow repeatedly with both their hands together close to their mouths." Rafael replied, "That is awesome." But this is where it becomes tricky. Manolo never asked neither Rafael nor Josefina about their summer. They had taken a trip to Croatia, which Manolo and the others knew about. *No había ni una pregunta de cortesía en el intercambio del diálogo socrático.* (There wasn't even a "courtesy" question asked in the Socratic exchange of the dialogue.)

Rafael's sister-in-law, Anastasia, insisted that it was alright not to respond to *preguntas* (questions) or ask *des questions*. Josefina had sent a group text to Anastasia and her children before their five o'clock gathering to head out to the plantation restaurant to celebrate their uncle and aunt's anniversary. Josefina wished them a happy Fourth of July and asked if they had received it. Anastasia cut her short by stating, "I don't respond to group texts." Now, talk about a conversation killer. In a previous exchange, Josefina and Rafael were concerned about Pepe, another nephew, who decided to drop out of a Physique/Bodybuilding competition for which he was training to participate in. Josefina *quería motivarlo* (wanted to motivate him) to follow his diet and stick with the plan. Rafael had also written Anastasia a text supporting Pepe and suggesting that it's normal to fear and doubt one's talents. All athletes experience this, but what's important is to follow through and to compete with oneself to overcome these hindering and debilitating obstacles. Rafael would have communicated this to him, but Pepe never responded to any of his texts in the past, whether it was wishing him a happy birthday or wishing him well in an athletic event he did years ago with his brother and stepfather. However, Anastasia never answered or responded to his text. As a result, it was *difficile* to try to engage her or her children in any type of normal or Millennial "parlance."

It seems like there is more to a family gathering than just expressing the superficial niceties of "How are you? It's so nice to see you?" After this type of informal parley, people usually sit by their immediate family members and do not interact with others, who have come in from out of town; whom they haven't seen in a long time—sometimes months or years. The art of conversation is a skill, one that is not taught in schools and in many families. It seemed apparent to Rafael that the only way to show an interest in people, whether they are *familia* or not, is to ask them "inquiries." He wondered if it was the narcissism of everyone that keeps him/her from asking questions.

He recollected a year or so ago, he and Josefina were visiting Anastasia and her late husband, Jaime, in Fresno, California. They were all sitting at the table after eating a nice breakfast consisting of eggs, bacon, and fresh fruit. Rafael had brought a copy of his latest book *Solitary Impressions*, which he kindly autographed and gave a copy to them. Jaime picked it up and looked at the back cover. Anastasia never looked at it, and Jaime quickly placed it back on the table and returned to his iPad. The book sat on the table the rest of the weekend without being touched. It was interesting to concur they were incapable of showing an interest or making any kind of comment. If someone would have given Rafael a book, he would have been delighted and would have at least asked about its content.

This behavior seemed very odd to Rafael, but he realized over the years that it was very common. Many people are maladroit at demonstrating an enthusiastic concern for others and in carrying on conversations. It's almost like most prefer to sit at a bar with a drink in hand watching a sporting event on the overhead TV and spouting out random comments about the game to the person next to them. It's an indirect conversation that most people favor. Is it the wall of narcissism that keeps people from interacting with one another?

CASTRO POINTS HIS MIDDLE FINGER AT LATINOS

THE FOLLOWING DAY Josefina and Rafael were perusing the *San Antonio Express-News* when they came across another interesting political article while sipping on their first cup of coffee brewed from their newly acquired Hamilton Beach coffee maker. It was beguiling to observe that Julián Castro is very vocal in his latest criticism of the current administration by stating that "Trump wants to replace the torch in the hand of the Statue of Liberty with a middle finger." My question is: "Isn't Castro pointing his middle finger at Latinos from Mexico, Central and Latin America, and the US by not speaking Spanish?"

I can substantiate my point because as an Anglo I grew up in San Juan, Puerto Rico. Unlike most Americans, who attended English speaking schools for fear of being bullied, oppressed, and singled out as minorities on the island, my sister and I attended Spanish public schools (Julio Sellés Solá and Sotero Figueroa) from the 3rd through the 9th grades. My parents had the foresight to realize this was the only way we would learn Spanish and become truly bilingual. Was I bullied by being the only Anglo kid with blond hair in school? Of course, I was, but I survived by holding my own with my fists and a nickel-plated belt buckle, the harsh "diplomatic tools" of junior high. Now, as an adult, the hardships outweighed the benefits of becoming a native speaker of Spanish and being able to navigate the intrinsic culture of the Hispanic community. I could truly communicate with Latinos in their native language with my intellect and not my fists. Sure, I could interface with Latinos in English, but, by communicating in Spanish, the relationship is truly authentic; a strong bond is established.

Castro's excuse for not learning Spanish: "In my grandparents and mother's time, Spanish was looked down upon. You were punished in school if you spoke Spanish." To me this is a cop-out for Castro and his twin brother, Rubén Navarrette, a Mexican-American journalist, and many others who had the same experience and support this view, which is popular among many Mexican Americans. What is surprising is that Castro's mother was a Chicana activist who fought against the oppression and racism towards Hispanics during the civil rights movement of the 60s. The irony here is that she was fighting for Chicanos who look different and speak Spanish. The Castro family assimilated learning English well, which is a good thing, but they painted over their Hispanic heritage by postulating as Anglos and not as Latinos or Mexican Americans by not learning Spanish.

What is baffling is that both Julián and Joaquín Castro studied Latin, Japanese, and German during their formative years. But why didn't they learn Spanish when they both realized at a young age that they wanted to serve the public politically? It is also equally astounding that they both graduated from Harvard and didn't learn Spanish. I think it's time for both to take a hiatus from American politics and move to a Central or Latin American country with their families to become truly fluent in Spanish. It's difficult for many to view Castro as a candidate who can truly ascertain the crisis on the border and the internal historical and political causes of Hispanics fleeing their native countries to come to the U.S. with a monolingual lens and with an Anglo mindset.

When Mexican Americans and other American Latinos decide not to learn Spanish and English well, it's a subtle form of racism. Of course, they can choose what language to learn, but if a person chooses to run for public office in the U.S., it seems logical to become bilingual in English and Spanish, the two dominant languages in America. Rafael was reminded of the drama *Vejigantes*, written by the late Puerto Rican writer Francisco Arriví, which describes the life of Cambucha, an African Puerto Rican who spreads white powder on her Black skin to acquire a whiter and clearer complexion. She also contemplates having surgery to reduce the size of her lips to attract the courtship of an American man. When the American comes over to visit her, she places her Black grandmother in the back room of the house so that the American can't see her. Cambucha wants to deny her Afro-Puerto Rican heritage because of the existing racism against Blacks in Puerto Rico and the U.S.

Josefina related Cambucha's predicament to that of Julián Castro, his twin brother Joaquín, and Rubén Navarrette, the popular Mexican-American journalist. They refused to learn Spanish, and all three graduated from Ivy League universities in the U.S. They escaped the Hispanic barrios from where they were raised to forget and abandon their roots. Basically, they use English to cover their skin color, but they use it to their advantage to criticize Trump and other Anglos to give themselves a political advantage. They pose as Hispanics when it is advantageous for seeking votes for the presidency as is the case with Julián Castro. They deceive those who only see their skin color but not their souls. A true Hispanic or in this case, a Mexican American, running for office should respect his legacy and culture by being bilingual in both, English and Spanish.

It was another early morning with both Josefina and Rafael sitting at their dining room table in their yellow sunroom savoring the early light of summer filtering through the numerous windows. Their cat, Garmo, was sitting on the grey and white fenced ledge of the backdoor steps leading to the wooden deck outside. Earlier, while the sprinklers were watering the shrubs and trees in the backyard, a skunk rummaged along the plants and foliage along the fence line enjoying the coolness of the morning and the spattering water refreshing his *trigueña* (golden skin) and Black and white coat as he frolicked in and out of the greenery. They were fortunate enough to take the time for prayer and thankfulness for their lives and the blessings they both had been granted over the years. For Rafael, it was a privilege to be able to write and contemplate life. By drafting and carving words on pages, he was able to connect with his spirit on a regular basis to listen to God and to discern the areas in his life that needed attention. Instead of becoming idle or becoming immersed in mindless activities every day, it gave him a serendipitous moment to observe and record his thoughts.

IMMIGRATION AND POLITICAL DISCORD

AS "JARS OF clay" he agreed with Josefina that they needed to be reshaped and molded each day to adapt and exist in a world that is constantly evolving. Writing allowed him to pause and detach himself from the frantic pace of life in the attempt to not only "commiserate" with himself but with the lives of others as well. Lately, he thought about the "ulterior motive remarks" of President Trump who was the center of another controversy. He tweeted to four women of color who serve in Congress: "Go back to the countries you came from." Trump is evidently frustrated by comments these women have made in their concerted effort to try to impeach him for many of his policies, especially immigration, where thousands of children and adults are caged in cramped detention centers along the U.S. and Mexican border. It is evident that the crisis at the southern perimeter is horrific, but at the same time, many illegal immigrants from Mexico and Central America have entered the U.S. in the past and failed to return to court for their asylum cases. This drawback has been out of control for many years, and there is not an easy solution.

Josefina was appalled by how members of Congress, both Democrats and Republicans, try to blame each other. It is common practice for many to point fingers at each other calling one another a "racist." As a society, she believed it was incumbent to move past this type of name calling and accusations. The immigration conundrum like other salient concerns like terrorism and racism, for instance, must include a comprehensive analysis of history, culture, and global politics. The matter must not be isolated only to the idea of *enjaular* (to cage) o *no enjaular* children at the border. It's crucial to discuss the instability of Venezuela, for example, with Maduro's dictatorship starving its people and the international support for Mr. Guaidó who is vying to replace Maduro's rule. The influx of Venezuelan refugees to Brazil and Colombia is another "vexation" for those countries receiving them. The coca production was increased in Colombia even though the war against the FARC (Fuerzas Armadas Revolucionarias de Colombia-The Revolutionary Armed Forces of Colombia [People's Army]) has ended some eleven years ago. But other violent *pandillas* (gangs) have splintered since the government has delayed helping the rural communities rebuild after the devastation caused by the war. This is just a small example of the macrocosm of problems that affect each country in a global community. Obviously, the gangs and drug cartels in Mexico and Central America benefit from the cocaine production. It feeds their savage lifestyle and is the source of their subsistence. Plus, there are countries like Iran, China, and Russia that support Maduro and his dictatorship in Venezuela.

There is a constant struggle in our world between capitalism, socialism, and totalitarianism. All citizens and politicians of the world must be *au courant* about these struggles to see the quandaries not with narrow lenses but with wider ones. A possible initiative for attacking the stark conditions in Honduras, El Salvador, and Guatemala, for example, would be to send a coalition of armed military units from NATO to these countries to arrest and combat these *trincas* (street rings) that represent the rule of law in these countries. The military could arrest and take away their weapons; at the same time, they could work together with local politicians and civilians to build institutions to rehabilitate them. This way, former gang members could reenter society and succeed in obtaining legal jobs in which they could earn a livelihood and contribute to the well-being of society and their fellow citizens.

Recently, Sasha and Josefina shared a cup of steamy *café con leche* at the local coffee house on Broadway St. As the design of the cream on top dissipated after their second sip, their discourse centered on the "remarks and ulterior motives" of Ilhan Omar, the newly elected democratic representative from Minnesota. A native Muslim of Somalia raised in the U.S., Omar stated Muslims were the victims of the 9/11 attack in New York and also retorted that "some group" attacked the twin towers that killed approximately 3,000 people of all nationalities. Sasha wondered whether Omar, a Muslim, was defending the Islamic jihadist terrorist attack by not naming the Al-Qaeda group directly. One must question her motives and thinking when making such careless statements. There is obviously a mistrust of the Islamic community in the United States and rightly so. It's not to say that all Muslims are jihadists, but it seems like many American Muslims don't speak out sufficiently against the evil of these extremists who promote global terrorism.

According to Josefina, Omar has had the privilege of being elected to Congress, which is a distinctive fortuity afforded to her by the people of the United States. This is a unique political position that probably never would have been an option for her in her native country of Somalia. She was raised in the U.S., an imperfect country, but in comparison to Somalia it would be rated on a scale closer to perfect than imperfect. If she lived in Somalia and criticized the government there, she would probably be jailed. Sasha believed Omar's divisive rhetoric represents her immaturity and narrow vision as a Somali American. There is no doubt that racism against the Muslims in the U.S. is a reality, and many are probably treated as second-class citizens. But this is not the proper way to discuss racism by not admitting that the 9/11 attack was carried out by a jihadist Muslim group.

Omar should acknowledge this as well as the American Muslim community at large must do as well. To overlook this fact is to misrepresent the American people of all ethnic backgrounds. How can Omar elucidate on the border crisis and the deplorable detention conditions housing women, men, and young infants from Mexico and Central American countries when she can't opine honestly about the events of 9/11 by inculpating and placing "onus" on the Islamic jihadist? It's easy to point the finger at the White establishment in the U.S. and blame them for many of the contentious issues when dealing with immigration and the events of 9/11.

Sasha was not surprised by Omar's declamations since she is young, and it is common to view things from one's specific ethnic background.

C'est difficile, whether one is Muslim, Jewish, or Christian and whether one is Black, White, or Hispanic, to view issues, especially racial ones, from the perspectives of others. This is a "thorny" conundrum that divides many Americans as well as many other people from divergent nations around the world. If we examine Sharia law, we learn that the word "sharia," means path to water. It is a legal code of law established by the Koran and the Prophet Muhammad that instructs Muslims on how to live an ethical, spiritual, and law-abiding life. However, it becomes bothersome, for example, when Sharia law, according to some interpretations, grants the courts in many Middle Eastern to give their henchmen the *luz verde* (green light) to flog, imprison, or decree a death penalty for homosexuals. Under Sharia law the death penalty may also be imposed on fornicators outside of marriage. How do we accept and discuss Sharia law when it opposes the Christian view in which *Jésus-Christ* merits life and pardons homosexuals and lesbians? In the U.S. the LGBT community is protected by the laws and rights of the U.S. Constitution. This is good, and it is a right in the U.S. that is not honored in many nations around the world. But we must also realize that many Muslim global communities in the Middle East see the rights of homosexuals and lesbians, as espoused in the U.S. and other countries, as an assault on their culture and Sharia law.

Sasha and Josefina agreed there is racism in the U.S. and other countries against Muslims, and this is why all perspectives must be discussed openly. Omar should state her position regarding the extremes of the Muslim faith. Does she support the jihadists in their contempt for American values and laws, one being the protection of the LGBT community? The issues fueling racism must not be sidestepped if there is to be an open dialogue to grow and surpass this cancer that affects the American public and the rest of the world. Is Omar adding to the fire and "senseless partitions" of America while calling President Trump a racist for stating she should return to her native country if she is against the values of the U.S. Constitution? There is no doubt Trump utters some idiotic things and stirs the "caldron of separateness" among Americans from an ethnic, racial, and religious point of view. But let's not fall into the trap of pointing fingers and labelling one another as intolerable bigots. Let's rise above this harmful rhetoric and discuss our dissensions and the combative issues *qui nous divisent* (separates us) and the things that divide us in a way that is peaceful, remittable, and uniting. To do this, one must be willing to look at one's own faith to see its faults as well as its virtues to question its positive as well as negative effects on our society. Omar must show more maturity in verbalizing the evil of the jihadist movement that promoted terrorism and death on 9/11 and other atrocities across the world to differentiate between Muslims who are radicals and non-radicals. To neglect to do so only adds to the heated kettle of visceral segregation in America and throughout the world towards Muslims in general. Omar should rise above the pettiness of American politics in which women pit themselves against the injustices imposed upon them by men, and Muslims and Christians label one another as xenophobes. These are "weighty" topics to cordially debate and defend, but as a House Representative, Omar and others should seriously address both sides of an argument to better serve the nation.

BICYCLES AND THE SPIRITUAL AND POLITICAL ROADS LESS TRAVELLED

RAFAEL REMINISCED ABOUT his bicycle ride yesterday on the farm roads east of Cibolo and IH-10 joining San Antonio to Houston, Texas. The asphalt was already warming quickly as he prepared his new trek Madone Speed bicycle and spread on his sunscreen. Putting on sunscreen was a process and a necessary evil that he applied meticulously to his face, nose, ears, and neck. Then, he proceeded to apply several layers of the sticky white film to both legs and arms covered mostly by his long sleeve jersey. He reapplied some more to his face before putting on his Oakley sunglasses. The wind was blowing at a good pace, probably about 12 mph. Today would be an easy ride since he averaged 19.1 mph two days ago covering 57.5 miles. He hoped to ride about 50 miles at a comfortable pace.

Lately, he'd been riding the same course out and back. He would ride for about 27 or 28 miles out and then turn around. At times the familiar route became boring with the same vibrations in the uneven asphalt with layers upon layers of corn fields and baled haystacks resting on the ground. But what he liked about this area was there was very little traffic, so it made it a safer ride. His route followed a zigzag path changing for stretches of three to four miles. Trees lined most of the road especially as he rode through Zuehl, Texas, a very small community with a saloon, church, cemetery, and the former Clemens School, which now served as a memorial and event center. He remembered stopping on the side of the road in late spring by the cemetery to fill his water bottles with water from a hose there and finding $60.00 spread across the grass in two twenties, one ten, and two five-dollar bills. At the same time, a man stopped his utility truck and offered him a cool and fresh bottle of Gatorade. It was a generous and hospitable gesture that is not frequently experienced in today's world, where people are rushing around to get from one place to another. He was also thankful for the money but felt some remorse for the person who lost it. He felt a need to possibly donate it to someone or to distribute the money to people on the street who needed food or something to drink.

The sun blazed through brown cornstalks, which had already been harvested, and warmed his body as he pedaled along. An occasional squirrel would cross his path, and he would recall the time one ran under his front wheel. He had to really hold on to his handlebars as he unexpectedly ran over it. It was a close call because he almost spilled over onto the blacktop, but luckily, he was able to maintain his balance. The squirrel unfortunately was not as fortunate as it twitched, but seemed to still be alive, even though it was probably severely injured and would die. He felt terrible about hitting it, but he reminded himself that it was unintentional. On a brighter note, he enjoyed stopping when he spotted a turtle in the middle of the road trying to go from side to another. He would pick it up with one or two hands, depending on its size, and place it safely in the grass on one side or another of the road. It was enjoyable to see it retract into its shell as it sought protection from me as I lifted it up. Thoughts would come and go as the shadows of tractors passed by going to the hayfields: the U.S., Texas, and Longhorn flags flew from fence posts, tall weeds grew from the sides of the roads, lonely hawks soared in the distance, the occasional outer shell of an armadillo decorated the roadside, and the black spots of tar soft from the sun's heat filled numerous potholes.

As he rode his thoughts turned to Scott Peck's book *The Road Less Traveled*. He seemed to like to return to this classic many times, especially when he needed finding a new book to read. It provided him with much food for thought. Peck believed that one could not separate psychology from spirituality. Rafael mused over the point Peck makes about taking responsibility for solving one's own contentious matters. Many times, a person blames himself or others for metaphysical "quagmires" he doesn't want to face on his own. Peck presents a case of a friend who felt like he was oppressed by police officers during the 1960s because of his long hair. Instead of dealing with the self-quandary, he preferred to complain and not do anything about it. He could obviously have moved to another part of the country where people were more tolerant of this hairstyle, or he could have chosen to cut it. Finally, he could have acknowledged that not all police officers felt this way about elongated and protracted tresses, but instead he chose to remain a victim of this injustice by the choice he made.

Taking responsibility for solving our inner dilemmas is burdensome; it is something we must continue to do for the rest of our lives according to Peck. We, as humans, obviously have the freedom to face our predicaments and choose to solve them or ignore them. By disregarding them, our lives become more conflictive and less harmonious. Once we accept the fact that life is difficult and requires us to confront and solve our misfortunes, life becomes easier and less of a struggle according to Peck.

Rafael also believed if we surrendered our lives personally to God, we realize that we do have the responsibility to resolve our own individual vexations; we are not alone in this process. God naturally wants us to internalize singly as we navigate through the drawbacks imposed by our predicaments. We, as human beings, all face *enigmas desconcertantes* (disconcerting) that we must "accost" and attempt to solve.

Recently, Rafael thought about the political climate in Puerto Rico where thousands of citizens took to the streets protesting the corruption and scandals of Governor Ricardo Rosselló's Cabinet that squandered money stockpiling millions of dollars in debt. The economy of the island has been suffering now for a decade due to the mismanagement of money given to private companies and firms that have not invested in education and improved the electrical infrastructure of the country, which was furthered damaged by Hurricane Maria in 2017. The U.S. Federal Government is now overseeing how money is distributed to help rebuild the electric infrastructure of the island. Most of the population wants Rosselló to resign, especially after uncovering the sexist and unprofessional emails shared among him and members of his Cabinet making fun of homosexuals, like the singer and songwriter, Ricky Martin, and calling some women in politics whores. Furthermore, they also made fun of the dead who were victims of the devastating Hurricane Maria. This is the largest protest ever organized in Puerto Rico since it became a U.S. territory at the end of the Spanish American War in 1898 and then became a Commonwealth (Estado Libre Asociado) in 1952. The crisis in Puerto Rico represents a government that has not taken responsibility for solving its problems, but the citizens are now taking control by voicing their discontent and pleading for Rosselló's resignation, which is a step in the right direction. Many citizens in other countries would be content with ignoring the problem and stating this is how it has always been. The corruption within the government cannot be changed, and this lackadaisical attitude predominates in Mexico and in many Central and Latin American countries. As a result, an immigration crisis at the border of the U.S. and Mexico is brewing and worsening each day.

Rafael learned that Governor Ricardo Rosselló did submit his resignation, and his final day in office was August 2, 2019. It's amazing that the Puerto Rican people marched peacefully protesting his leadership, and Rosselló stepped down without any violence or deaths among the protesters. However, it will be difficult to find someone to replace him at this time since the people are also demanding that his staff be dismissed and superseded as well. At least, Rosselló did the right thing by resigning, which represents a step in the right direction for the island. Puerto Rico has had the good fortune of being a Commonwealth of the U.S. since 1952, which has allowed it to receive federal aid like social security and other grant money for improving its educational infrastructure. Lately, the island has received federal money to help pay for the destruction caused by Hurricane Maria in 2017. But this aid package was not managed properly; as a result, it did not get into the hands of the proper organizations and companies for rebuilding the out-of-date electrical power system, the schools, and many residences that were destroyed. The dishonesty of politicians and other governmental officials always leads to corruption and misappropriation of government funds.

As Rafael and Josefina thought about the affairs of the world and of their individual lives, they agreed with Peck who discusses the significance of openness and honesty in this printed work *The Road Less Traveled*. Rafael found himself returning to the worn pages of this book repeatedly. He concurred with Peck that it is a never-ending burden of self-discipline for us, as humans, to attempt to be honest and open. Those that speak the truth, according to Peck, are secure in knowing they have done nothing to contribute to the confusion of the world. Instead, they have served as beacons of illumination and clarification. When we are dedicated to the truth, we live in the "transparent;" this allows us to become free from fear due to the courage we have exercised.

Josefina came to the realization that as "jars of clay" we are molded by our circumstances and by God when we can sit alone for long periods of time. In her sixties now, she became self-cognizant of time standing still just enough to cause some anxiety. The disquiet stemmed from the fact she felt compelled to remain busy with chores and existential and non-existential chattels scratched off from the infamous "to do list." Sitting still to think and write was arduous and uncomfortable. She had to take that time to avow the "clay" that God, with his love, uses to mold the "jar," the representation of her life and the lives of all mankind. For as Peck explicates in his writings, one must suffer greatly to experience joy. As humans, we want to cushion ourselves from agony, and when we do so, we no longer grow. For example, it is easier not to *escribir* than to write; however, when one forces oneself to *écrire*, one experiences joy. Love and joy are synonymous just like openness and honesty. Peck defines love: "It is the will to extend oneself for the purpose of nurturing one's own or another's spiritual growth." He also states that when we love someone, it becomes demonstrable or true only through our exertion. We take an extra step or go the extra mile for that person. Peck concludes that love requires effort, and it is not quiescent.

Rafael agreed with Josefina wholeheartedly, and as they continued through the journey of life together, they realized that maintaining a *cariñosa* (tenderly caring) relationship after ten years requires effort. When he was young, he often idealized marriage as a bond between two people who were older and wiser. He visualized everything being perfect and painless once one reached a certain age of maturity. What he didn't realize in youth, now, that he was 61 years old, is that life is a journey between birth and death; it doesn't get easier, but with each passing day and year, there is an "juncture" to grow in love. It is easier to live a mindless existence as one ages. Rafael thought of two of his sister's roommates who share a home together for people with disabilities, whether they are physical or mental health related. Rafael thought of the endless hours the house companions, Pablo and Beatriz, spent sitting in their garage mindlessly smoking and watching television. Rafael still had compassion and *amour tendre* (tender love) for them because they were humans in need of love just as he was. Their existence made him question his *raison d'être* and its meaning. What could possibly be going through their minds, day to day? As an observer, Rafael wanted to think about their lives and histories as he pondered his being and experiences. We all choose, and Rafael like Josefina wanted to be a "wordsmith" and meditate on love, joy, suffering, birth, death, and transcendence. Writing was their medium for creating and contemplating much like the potter who molds "terracotta" into jars. The catlinite represents the words, and the jars are the end-product or books.

It was another quiet morning interrupted by the revolving dryer in the kitchen. The coffee was crisp and full as Rafael took a sip from his favorite *España* cup. He watched the second debate last night between the Democratic candidates running for the 2020 presidential election. It was interesting to listen to them wanting to tax the rich, discuss the damage caused to the environment by fossil fuels, racism, and the tariff wars against China. Plus, they also dialogued about pulling out the military from the long-lasting war in Afghanistan, which has now persisted for almost 19 years. It seemed like they all harshly debated the same concerns without any new vantage points on nagging "troubles" affecting us domestically and internationally. Many, if not all, blamed President Trump for the inflamed schism and racism that has ignited and initiated more acts of home-grown terrorism in our country, supposedly, the culprit being the far-right White supremacists' groups.

Both Republicans and Democrats view our problems from a simplistic lens. It is easy to castigate President Trump for "senseless partitions" based on his harsh words in which he recently told three congresswomen, one a Muslim and the other two of color, to return to their country of origin. We all know Trump says some idiotic and infantile pronouncements all the time, which are offensive and unexpected. But, as a mature nation, we must not dwell on this type of recalcitrant rhetoric. Intellectually and spiritually, we owe it to ourselves to rise above this pettiness to work on the extremely germane matters to help bridge our dissimilarities and restore the value of heterogeneity. This way we can create a peaceful and respectable environment where all Americans can thrive as a country connected to the rest of the world.

WORLD CITIZENS

JOSEFINA AND SASHA were taking a walk last Saturday along the Salado Creek Greenway Trail here in San Antonio, and they both agreed with Ortega y Gasset, the *madrileño* (inhabitant of Madrid) author, who declared we must become *ciudadanos del mundo* (citizens of the world). This means we must always see ourselves in relationship to others, not just in America but with the rest of the world. For example, we must view the past-horrific institution of slavery in America, which is now eradicated, but continues as an enterprise still practiced in many parts of the world today. It is represented in the form of forced labor among children in places like Africa, the worldwide-sex trade and exploitation of minors, and the *trincas* (street rings) from Central America forcing minors to join their *pandillas*.

Democrats and Republicans, for the most part, are disconnected from the world at large and the Latino community in the United States since they view "arguments" from the "American" point of view. There is a discordance between the many politicians who graduate from Ivy League universities like Yale, Harvard, Princeton, Stanford, and multiple others. Graduates from these universities usually gravitate to the Left politically, socially, and economically. They rally for civil rights for all people, but they really don't connect with Latinos or African Americans.

They are enamored with wanting to help; they often deliberate about the significance of reparations for Black ancestors of the slave population. The far Left send their children to Paris to visit the Louvre or to Spain to peruse *Museo del Prado*. They stare and admire the Mona Lisa and talk about the exploits of Leonardo Da Vinci, or they glare at the stark-dark eyes of El Greco's painting, *El caballero,* with his elongated fingers and eyes focused melancholily towards heaven. The Ivy Leaguers take Spanish, French, and German courses to fulfill their degree requirement, but remain monolingual, only remembering a few catch phrases like, *"Más cervezas, ¿Dónde está el baño?, Adiós Trump, y Estoy postulando ser el próximo presidente de los Estados Unidos* (I am 'posing' to become the next president of the United States.)".

According to Rafael and his friends, monolingualism in America is its downfall. Its comprehension of complex political problems in the Middle East, Russia, Europe, and other countries is limited to the insights and translations only provided by interpreters and google. Rafael had just finished reading an article, "The Downside of Diversity," by Anthony Kronman, a Sterling Professor of Law at Yale University and a former dean of Yale Law School, was published August 3, 2019 in the Wall Street Journal. He basically stated that the agenda of diversity, the hot topic among all university campuses throughout the U.S., is a political motive. This is to say it's not acceptable for a member of a minority group, such as an African American, to speak out in favor of reforming the "seeming less irreparable botherations (aggravations)" in the inner cities of America where violence predominates among Black gangs. The focus is always on police brutality, which pits the White police officer against the Black offender. In other words, according to Kronman, it is no longer the truth, which is valued in discussions across college campuses in the U.S., and neither is independent thinking esteemed to find the root cause of racial tensions and prejudices between ethnic groups. Not only is this a problem, but what Kronman fails to comprehend is that the debate about the significance of diversity is limited to the commonality of monolingualism throughout the institutions of higher education in the U.S. Mr. Kronman is a victim of this opium-monolingual intellectualism as well.

To become an independent thinker, according to Rafael and his friends, it's necessary to speak or attempt to speak another language to be sentient to a disparate perspective. If one were to speak French and travel to France, for example, it would be possible to talk to the French in their native language about their views on multifariousness and truth. Do their ideas differ from those in the U.S.? Kronman contradicts himself in this essay by stating that Tocqueville believed independent-mindedness is the antidote to the "tyranny of majority opinion." *C'est la verité* (truth). However, Kronman is presenting this vantage point from the American point of view, not a worldly understanding. This is a common mistake among many of the American professors across the U.S. In their attempt to present a unique, aberrant, and independent viewpoint, they support a concept that is common to many in academia who peruse complex concerns from an American and English monochrome only "spectrum."

Many would be in awe and deem Kronman's essay on diversity as a sophisticated and intellectual outlook since he teaches at Yale. Yale is an Ivy League university; therefore, it is one of the top think tanks of academia not only in the U.S. but widely recognized throughout the world. As a result, Professor Kronman's conviction should represent the *crème de la crème* of American thought and intellectualism. However, the opposite is true. It's like saying one is an expert in the art of tasting ice cream, but one is only familiar with savoring vanilla. Kronman is in a position of privilege, teaching at Yale University, and many would consider his writings a symbol of acute-critical thinking.

Rafael was sitting at the Hyatt Hotel in Austin, Texas waiting for Josefina who was attending a conference on endocrinology for the last few days. He looked over the balcony of his room facing Town Lake and reminisced about his years spent in graduate school at the University of Texas in the late 1980s. The twelve-mile trail along the river remained moderately the same extending from the West Side to the East Side of IH-35. He remembered the intellectual snobbishness of many of the professors here who were hired to research and publish with a secondary emphasis on teaching. He recalled one class taught by a Latin American professor from Argentina who always wore a suit and a tie. He couldn't remember his name, but Rafael felt uncomfortable because the professor esteemed him as being an inferior student, not deserving to be in graduate school, especially at the University of Texas, which was viewed by many to be comparable to Harvard. The class focused on the Hispanic literature of

Latin America with an emphasis on Positivism, a philosophical concept founded by Auguste Comte at the beginning of the Industrial Revolution in the 19th century. The professor spoke eloquently with his Argentine fluency flowing from the *Versos sencillos* of José Martí to Luis Borges, the Argentine literary giant, who gained famed for his many writings, one being a categorization of a library with its resources of information and literature stacked neatly into an organization only capable of a European country, such as Spain. The higher intellectual capabilities of Europeans correlated to their diet, which consisted of beef, wheat, and superior food. Asian people relied primarily on rice, and the Indigenous populations of Latin America consumed corn, which were deemed to be the nutritional staples of inferior races. How could this "former *inferior* culinary staple of corn," deemed more nutritional than white-bleached flour today, fuel the intellectually-ignorant acuity of the Spaniards and other Europeans who wrongly considered themselves superior in their snobbery to these foregoing Indigenous cultures of historical yesterday? This was a "metaphorical code word" for the savant-dumb ambiance and haughtiness prevalent in the Department of Spanish and Portuguese where Rafael was pursuing a doctorate degree in Hispanic literature at the University of Texas.

Yesterday Rafael went to Barton Springs as he reminisced about the time he lived in Austin from the fall of 1987 until the summer of 1991. He parked on a dusty parking lot a quarter of a mile from the natural spring where the water temperature remained at 68 degrees. After securing and tying his truck key to the draw strings of his black jammer TYR (competitive designer and manufacturer of competitive triathlon apparel, named after the mythological Norse god, Týr), he proceeded to put on his wetsuit. Then, he meticulously applied sunscreen to his face, legs, and arms. The natural pool was replete with people swimming, floating on inflatable devices, and sunbathing. He remembered more than twenty years ago studying for his psycholinguistics final exam. It was almost like yesterday sensing that the trees and dry grass around the pool remained unscathed and the same. The men's open-aired changing area with bathrooms and showers were untouched. The fresh green water was invigorating as he swam up and down numerous times to complete an hour swim. The clear water with a rocky bottom was flawlessly unaffected, and the squeaky diving board was still clanking. He evoked the soothing memory of sitting on his towel years ago reading his book and taking notes. Today Rafael dodged miniature floating rafts with people holding on, swimmers crossing from side to side, and people wallowing in the shallow water. It was natural with women in thong swimsuits with shapely butt cheeks exposed. It was Austin with its natural, easy, and peaceful "groove." Even the "birds" walked in their halter tops with their leather sandals with that special sway and cornucopia of tattoos on their backs, arms, and legs. I mean it was the home of the legend, Stevie Ray Vaughan, whose bronze statue still decorates the "cool" but renowned cinder and dirt running path at Zilker Park in Austin, Texas—the cornerstone of the Lone Star State known for being liberally and politically "Weird."

This "so called '**coolness**'" is a very ignorant and "monolingually" deficient trait of many Austinites who are known for their "dead brain aloofness." This state of no-mind Zen describes most Americans who are globally incompetent when referring to and dealing with the 2024 complex international concerns in which President Biden and Vice President Harris basically support Hamas in Israel because of their failed policies with open borders in Texas with Mexico, for example. The Biden-Harris team blindly, idiotically, and willingly greenlight and champion their extreme liberal, cultural, and political agenda.

The Biden Administration encourages the trafficking of young children, as they coordinate and "sleep" with the Mexican Drug Cartels and the new Mexican President Claudia Sheinbaum, to pedophiles in the United States and across the nations of the world. Kamala Harris still has no clue regarding the international dilemmas and complexities of the modern global societies and people of the today. This explains why Harris lost *avergonzadamente* (ashamedly) on election day in November 2024.

On Thursday night Josefina and Rafael walked across the Congress Avenue Bridge on their way to the iconic Sixth Street, the "Live Music Capital of the Texas" with a line on both sides of the street stacked with bars and music. The genres extended from jazz, blues, classical, reggae, rock-n-roll, and everything in between. A street person brought his ten-foot yellow boa constrictor for display. Two seminude girls danced on two open windowsills of one of the bars. They finally settled in Friends, a blues bar, where Austin Cobb, a young teenager was playing riffs from his electrical *guitarra*. The scene hadn't changed for the past 30 years. Rafael bought a Lone Star Light Lager as he and Josefina listened to the dexterity of the young musician with his fingers dancing on the strings of his string *guitare* instrument. This was Austin where it was still *chévere* (hip) to hang out, drink a *cerveza*, and listen to music. The tune of "Mustang Sally" resonates today as it did so many years ago clearing the cobwebs of his memory.

THE MOLDING OF CLAY AND THOUGHTS

THE "JARS OF clay" of the past became the clay of the present. As he sat in the atrium of the hotel lobby, people came by rolling their suitcases along the carpeted corridor. This manuscript was a work of meditation on life and for a continual search for meaning as more than two decades had gone by since he lived in Austin. It is a reflection on work, society, local and global politics, culture, relationships, philosophy, and many other "jars." Rafael believed it was necessary to think, observe, and reflect. He didn't want to live life each day in semiretirement not creating. He desired to take his personal pipestone to mold it into jars of memories and recollections. By thinking about Liberals and Conservatives, he could view the inconsistencies and contradictions in both political and philosophical spectrums. Socrates espoused the notion that there is a difference between one's opinion and the truth. A person may have formed a strong conviction about a viewpoint or experience he is very familiar with, but this does not mean he understands the complete *la verdad* (verify) of this subject. For example, Rafael grew up in San Juan, Puerto Rico and speaks fluent Spanish, but he does not hold the complete truth or understanding of the island's culture and language compared to someone who knows nothing about Puerto Rico.

The stream of consciousness style suited Rafael because thoughts flow through our minds during all the moments of our waking and sleeping hours. He anticipated his high school class reunion to take place August 31-Sept. 2 in Winter Park, Florida. The other night he dreamt of his senior class trip to some beach cabins in Jobos, Puerto Rico on the northwestern coast of the island. He recalled sitting in front of the ocean on a magical morning at 2 a.m. with Hortensia. They had just made out, and they were talking about relationships. He had a steady girlfriend a year younger who did not come to this trip with his *compañeros*. Rafael felt like he betrayed her and wanted to talk to Hortensia about it. The rocky ocean and waves slammed on the *sable* (sand) in front of them. The moonlight frolicked in front of them reflecting in their eyes as they spoke to one another. They were two adolescents meditating and musing about love and couples. This represented the seed of many liaisons to come for them both. They would grow and mature over the years, and they would learn valuable lessons about lovers, friends, family, and anonymous members of society.

As Rafael pondered the beginning of this manuscript with Marcos and Sasha with the volcanic scene along the San Marcos River, he thought about an appropriate ending. His thoughts were interrupted by the mass shooting in El Paso, Texas where a young gunman of 21 years of age, Patrick Crusius, drove from Dallas to a Walmart near the border of El Paso and Ciudad Juárez and opened fire with an assault weapon killing at least twenty people and leaving more than thirty wounded on August 3, 2019, in the late morning hours. Less than 24 hours later Connor Betts opened fire at the historic Oregon District of Dayton, Ohio killing nine people with an "AR-15 like" assault rifle with magazines containing 100 rounds. He was shot to death by police in less than a minute after the barrage had started. Connor, who was 24 years, shot his sister, Megan, 22, and her male friend first. They had driven together to the district and then went their separate ways. Megan died while her companion survived and was being treated at a nearby hospital.

After meditating on the murder of Megan by her brother Connor, Rafael thought about the murder of Abel by his brother Cain in the Bible. Cain was jealous because God looked with favor on Abel and his offerings but did not look favorably on Cain. After Cain murdered Abel, the Lord told Cain that the soil he worked would not yield a crop, and he would become a restless wanderer. There was no capital punishment forthcoming then for murder. Why did Rafael contemplate this biblical story in relation to the death of Megan by her brother Connor? Not only did Connor senselessly murder innocent people, but he also took the life of his sister. We, the survivors, are left to try to infer with reason his motive and piece together this tragic puzzle. Josefina reminded Rafael that we are all "jars of clay," which are molded by society and culture. The political climate created by both Democrats and Republicans is one of division and racism. Young minds, like Connor and Patrick's, are influenced by the internet and hate groups, pitting Whites against Hispanics and Blacks and vice versa. God warned Cain that he must master sin because it "was crouching at his door." Sin overwhelmingly mastered Cain when he murdered Abel.

Rafael opined our society had drifted away from prayer and meditation. Our children and youth, in many instances, are left defenseless with the abundance of malicious evil on the internet and mindless video games in which good and bad obliterate each other. Love is the key, *el amor* can only spread when in *la sociedad* (society) we dialogue and place our dissimilarities on the table. America needs leaders that can navigate the vicissitudes of divergent cultures and races. Josefina and Rafael acknowledged we must reshape society like a potter molding new jars of clay. The political pointing of fingers between the Democrats and Republicans is the cause of many of the ills in America along with the silence of our churches afraid to take a stand against the name-calling and labeling. Today Rep. Joaquín Castro posted online the names and employers of 44 prominent San Antonio donors to President Trump. He retorted these individuals fueling Trump's hate campaign labeling Hispanic immigrants as "invaders," suggesting this rhetoric influenced the shooter who carried out the mass shooting in El Paso this weekend. The gunman posted a hate filled manifesto online warning of a "Hispanic invasion of Texas." Castro identified the donors as Balous Miller, owner of the Bill Miller BBQ restaurant chain, Christopher "Kit" Goldsbury, developer of the Pearl Entertainment District, and Realtor Phyllis Browning. They each donated $5,600 to Trump, which is the maximum allowable contribution to a single candidate. This type of infantile pointing of fingers by Castro also feeds into the racism that America is experiencing, and it adds fire to the flame of venomous rancor instead of extinguishing it.

THE INITIAL DREAM

RAFAEL RETURNED TO his dream at the beginning of this manuscript. He envisioned a volcano erupting, and from its depths he witnessed a grassroots movement, one that was all inclusive. The United States was disintegrating from within the fire of the volcano's mouth, and from the ashes people were emerging with a new vision. They joined with other people from other countries and continents (Iran, North Korea, Guatemala, Syria, and underdeveloped nations), which were also crumbling. It was a global renaissance occurring in every country on the face of the earth. The emerging people brought their own clay, and they set out to mold jars representative of the new United Countries of the World. Everyone would have a voice in electing and choosing a governing body.

There would still be three branches of government: legislative, judicial, and executive. It would be like the United States, but it would be all encompassing and inclusive of all the nations of the world. The borders separating countries would merge; dictators and oppressive governments would be overruled and ousted by the majority. Rich and powerful organizations like the NRA would not influence policy and the drafting of new laws. There would be a constitution that values and underscores *la diversité* and the respect for all languages, ethnic groups, cultures, and their heritages. Learning multiple languages would be strongly encouraged even though it wouldn't be an absolute to learn them.

Josefina, Sasha, Marcos, and their other friends knew that it wouldn't be a perfect government, but it would be one that attempted to design a world in which there was less poverty, violence, and illegal activities. Domestic as well as international terrorism would be monitored and eliminated. Instead of voting for a single president or leader for each country, the population of individual nations, like the U.S., for example, would vote for a commission of five people including men and women representative of the ethnic makeup and tapestry of the North American society: Hispanics, Whites, African Americans, Asians, and many other minorities. They would have to reach an accord on all contentiously controversial points regarding immigration, weapons, trade, terrorism, health care, and the eradication of child trafficking through open boarders, primarily with the licentiously decadent malfeasance of the Mexican government and the new presidential administration of Claudia Steinbaum, which "secretively" colludes with the Mexican drug Cartels.

Furthermore, the Biden-Harris democratic-liberal machine, which is completely monolingual and culturally ignorant of Mexico's history, would fail because it is extremely clueless of the rest of Latin America historically, linguistically, and intellectually and of any other foreign nation globally.

The Biden-Harris-Alejandra Ocasio's farcical team, the heartbeat of the Liberal Democratic Party, now four years running with Harris presenting herself in the 2024 presidential election, seeks to be chosen by *la gente* as the first Black female president of the United States. It is astonishing to note the Democratic slogan preached by the Harris cohorts is: "If you don't vote for me, you ain't Black." This is the most asinine utterance ever expressed by a presidential candidate of any ethnic background demonstrating the imbecile intellect of a two-year old at most.

To add fuel to the incandescent fire, one should never forget the Obamas as being the worse bigots and hypocrites speaking in favor of minorities. However, they acted negatively by drafting policies against Blacks and Hispanics at levels unheard of in the short history, since its inception in 1776, of North America. They are completely juxtaposed to Martin Luther King Jr. who professed *Jesucristo* as the ultimate Savior and beacon of hope and light for a true Democracy for all American citizens, regardless of race or ethnic background and all-inclusive *filosofía* (philosophy) for all people globally. King also wisely affirmed to judge a man/woman not by the color of his skin but by the quality of his character.

If a consensus were not agreed upon, a local directorate as well as an international board would have a voice in the decision. But the most relevant and significant voice would come from many of the citizens of the U.S. in this case or in instances involving other countries. Prisons across the world would be required to implement rehabilitation programs to help inmates reenter society with skills that would help them be productive citizens. They would be able to rejoin society if they did not remain a threat to others.

The renaissance envisioned by Rafael, his friends, and the metaphor of "jars of clay" would focus on the spiritual aspects of all people and nations of the world. All dilemmas, whether they involve relationships, crime, mental illness, poverty, and others, pertain to the darkness and evil that have overcome the soul of men and women. Whether a person is a Christian, Muslim, Buddhist, Jew, Hindu, or atheist is not the source of petulant vexation. The friction between religions and philosophies of life stem from the lack of love shared among all people. *L'amour* has been defined divergently by many, and seeking definitions is futile. God wants us to love our enemies as well as our families and neighbors. We must keep this sacred concept in the forefront of all arguments, especially when we disagree with one another. When a political leader, like President Trump, refers to immigrants as "bad hombres" or as "rapists," we must not overly react. Are these inappropriate comments? Yes, they are. However, for example, it is childish to fight back like the Congressman Joaquín Castro has done by publishing the names of prominent Trump supporters in San Antonio and accusing those donors of siding with Trump with his attack and purposeful message of hate against immigrants and Hispanics. Furthermore, the tit for tat of blaming Trump and his hyperbole for the mass shooting by a young White supremacist follower at a Walmart full of Hispanics in El Paso, Texas is another example that must be avoided. As a nation, we must rise above the finger pointing. Rafael believed that a deeper ill existed in society. The White supremacist groups have existed since the end of the Vietnam War in the early 1970s or earlier, and they have propagated this type of malicious *odio* (hate) against all races of color other than white. These White supremacists' websites on the internet along with any other corrosive online web pages must be monitored and eliminated. The only *tertulias* (conversational groups) that should be allowed are those that embrace love and respect for our fellow man. Differences of opinions regarding race and other matters should always be addressed in a civil and fervently compassionate manner.

The United States has come a long way since the days of slavery and segregation due to the positive results of the civil rights movement of the late 1960s and early 70s. Barack Obama, a Black president, served for two terms as president. This is unheard of in other countries of the world where racism against Blacks and other minorities, such as the Indigenous tribes of Latin America, is more salient and deep-rooted than in the U.S. Rafael and Josefina opined the U.S. and other countries have made substantial progress but still have a long way to go in improving race relations among its populations. Roadblocks still exist between the Left and Right comprised of Democrats and Republicans. A new political party must emerge from the ashes of a violently segregated schism begotten by the former mentioned parties. Ivy League universities are failing in their mission of educating the elite and the selected few underprivileged who enter their ivory towers of higher education. The Castro twins and the journalist Navarrette are examples of Mexican Americans who had the opportunity to attend Harvard by means of their hard work and academic accomplishments. They should be applauded for their accolades; however, they ignored and continue to dismiss their souls as Hispanics by not learning the Spanish language. Ironically, they pretend to understand the Hispanic mind and culture. Without knowing Spanish, you can't travel to Lima, Perú, for example, and communicate with the people effectively, transparently, and culturally *en español* on *les rues* (streets) to hear their slant on life in their native countries or their perception and vantage point of the U.S. If one does not speak Spanish with some fluency, in this instance, one can't dialogue with presidents like Obrador from Mexico in their native language, the language that unites Mexicans and Hispanics. The Castros and Navarrette are "whiter" than President Trump, so to speak, because they don't speak Spanish. They are pretenders in their vein attempts to fool others into believing they are experts on matters involving Hispanics as well as other minorities because of the color of their skin. In Rafael's mind, this is the worst form of racism against one's own soul and the people the Castros and Navarrette are trying to represent, the Hispanic community. Trump's racial remarks are overt, but the Castros and Navarrette's biased discourse, for example, is subliminal but just as wrong.

The "jars of clay" represent all the people and cultures of the world. As humans Rafael knew that we had to open our souls to allow God in our lives. It's essential for people to sit still and silently search for God's voice to dialogue with Him. When we are open to our spiritual side, we are the clay God uses to shape us into a multitudinous myriad of types of jars. Josefina agreed with Rafael, but she conjectured that all of this is easier said than done. Periods of time in history, for example; people's convictions of one another change slowly. Rafael reminisced about his 40-mile bike ride last week while visiting the Saint Bernard Parish where Josefina's brother, Donosio, lives. They were there to attend their nephew's wedding. Along the road heading out towards Chalmette and St. Bernard State Park on Louisiana State Highway 39, he sensed the divide between Blacks and Whites in Louisiana. The grass was overgrown in many yards and many of the homes were in disarray. There was a sense of despair and indifference that still permeated the air as he passed the St. Bernard Prison. Racism still existed, but it was ignored and not discussed; thus, it was conveniently easier to evade as it corroded society in a very slow-bigoted-cancerous demise.

The inability to confer about and share divergent thoughts on racism and other contentious subjects are still major problematic "loopholes" in the U.S. and the world. American Liberals and Conservatives only focus on the wall and detention centers when pertaining to immigration, as an illustration; few refer to the manipulation of the Spaniards when they enslaved the Indigenous populations of the Olmecs, Aztecs, and Mayas. They further ignored the corruption of political parties like the Partido Revolucionario Institucional (PRI) in Mexico from 1921 to the present. The United Fruit Company from the U.S. also contributed to propagating the poverty in Central America by working side by side with dictators in the early to mid-twentieth century in generating wealth for themselves as they impoverished the working class. Speaking one language also limits journalists and other political representatives in comprehending difficult international issues. However, the most "sententious" concern is the spiritual divide that separates families, communities, and countries around the world.

Rafael had a vision in which the countries of the world would undergo a spiritual transformation so that all religions and cultures would embrace love, respect, and acceptance of all people, regardless of their race or ethnic background. Schools across the globe would include a curriculum on how to eliminate racism and build a world economy in which every country would participate in its development. There would be an international coalition that would monitor the Northern Central American Triangle (Honduras, El Salvador, and Guatemala), for example, uproot and eradicate the gangs and violence in those countries. The *pandilleros* (gang members) would be given a "vicissitude" to rehabilitate themselves and learn trades and job skills to reenter society to make an honest wage. Those who would not change would remain in *la cárcel* (jail) and be forced to work in agricultural or manufacturing areas. All schools would include children from all over the world thereby they could be exposed to a variant of ideas, languages, and ways of life. English could remain the dominant language, but all students would have to learn one or two more languages of their choice fluently. After middle school, students could choose to further their education with a college degree in mind, or they could enroll in a vocational or technological school. Every child would have to complete two courses in world history to recognize the historical dynamics that existed between countries; they would work together to comprehend the roots of racism in their homelands and across the world, finding solutions to end this *maladie* (sickness) and to make our world an all-inclusive one.

Although Rafael, Sasha, and their friends credited God and Jesus Christ as the true answers to all *les difficultés* of the world, they did not want Christians to force their faith on others. All religions and faiths would be accepted if they professed loving and treating everyone with equanimity. Fanatical religions and terrorism against others would not be tolerated. The intelligence agencies of the whole world would work together to extirpate and imprison these types of groups. They would be given the latitude to rehabilitate, but if this were not possible, they would be forced to work in manufacturing and agricultural farming positions while being incarcerated.

In Rafael's final dream, man would be given the *congruencia* (chance) to ask God in the initial garden of Adam and Eve: "Why do you not want us to eat from the tree of the forbidden fruit?" They would be able to question God not in a disrespectful manner but to establish a continual conversation with the Lord. A discourse that every man and woman from every nation of the world could have with Him. Men and women would come together to work, socialize, and pray together. God would provide every person with clay so they could shape "jars of clay." These *jarras* would be molded and formed as reminders that humans are fragile and break, but they can be reshaped and repaired with more clay. This is the inherently pertinent and fundamental dialogue each man needs to have with himself and others from around the globe. Rafael and his friends knew that people were becoming more and more isolated with the abundance of technology and the longer life span of humanity. Since people are living prolonged *vidas* (lives), they need to indulge in these philosophical and spiritual meditations because the churches throughout the world are not encouraging them to do so. Institutions, such as churches, schools, and universities, become stale and monotonous because they follow the same paradigm. Churches, for example, contain services with prayer, music, and sermons. These are good, but there is no room for questioning. A segment of each service should allow the congregation to *argumentar* (dialogue) on a certain subject, whether that be a discussion on existentialism according to Sartre, for example, and how does his philosophical discourse relate to the word of God?

Schools and universities should be more progressive by allowing students to dialogue amongst each other on topics, such as racism, sexism, politics, religion, and other numerous subjects. Lectures are still centered on the professor lecturing and leading the discussion. Students could discuss, e.g., *The Social Contract* by Rousseau and *The Republic* by Plato. Teachers and professors must pose these questions: How would you reshape our democracy? What can the educational system do to change and be more interactive with students playing a major role in their education? But, more consequentially, we need to feed the soul and ask students about their core values. We must inculcate in them the idea that they must *cuestionar* (to inquire) their ethereal inclinations. The spiritual life is the clay *que moldea las jarras* (pattern jars). Without this element there are no substances, and without the spirit there is no life worth living. God *a creé* (formed) all humans for a purpose, and we can only become truly human by examining, praying, growing, and evolving. Rafael agreed with Karl Jaspers, the German thinker, who stated: "The minister has found God and no longer searchers for Him, whereas the philosopher remains in a constant *BÚSQUEDA DE JESUCRISTO* (search)… for JESUS CHRIST" Rafael and Sasha wanted their search for God to continue indefinitely if there was enough clay to mold and "hand spin" more jars.